Oh No,
It's Sabbath
Again*

*And I'm Not Ready!

Oh No, It's Sabbath Again*

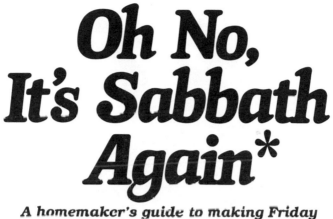

A homemaker's guide to making Friday the easiest day of the week.

*And I'm Not Ready!
Yara Cerna Young

Pacific Press Publishing Association
Boise, Idaho
Oshawa, Ontario, Canada

Edited by B. Russell Holt
Designed by Tim Larson
Cover by Lars Justinen
Typeset in 10/12 Bookman

Library of Congress Cataloging-in-Publication Data:

Young, Yara Cerna, 1954–
    Oh, no, it's Sabbath again, and I'm not ready! : a homemaker's
guide to making Friday the easiest day of the week / Yara Cerna
Young.
        p.   cm.
    ISBN 0-8163-1091-2
    1. Sabbath. 2. Home economics. 3. Child rearing—Religious
aspects—Seventh-day Adventists. 4. Seventh-day Adventists—
Doctrines. 5. Adventists—Doctrines. I. Title.
BX6154.Y67   1992
248.8'43—dc20   92-8170
                                                            CIP

92 93 94 95 96 • 5 4 3 2 1

Contents

Dedication

I dedicate this book to Jilma de Cerna, my mother. Without her example as a Christian wife, mother, and homemaker, this book would have never been written.

Foreword

Warning! This book could be dangerous to your daily routine!

In these pages, you'll discover some of the unique dynamics that make you tick when organizing your own home. And it may not always be a comfortable discovery. It's not always pleasant to have someone explain a better way of doing things or reveal your disorganization. It's at such a point, however, that Yara opens the door to order and wholeness, a sense of regaining control of your time and your life.

Let's face it. Most Sabbath-keeping women never begin worrying about Sabbath preparation before Thursday night. But according to Yara, we should be ready for Sabbath by Friday morning! In this book she will show you how she does it—and how you can do it too.

Yara's book focuses primarily on the nuts and bolts of home organization, establishing routines, and Sabbath preparation. But *why* is that so important for families today? Don't we have more important things to worry about than keeping the beds made and the dishes done? As a family-life educator and a home economist, I'm convinced that families who follow a simple plan of routine and organization are stronger families.

Some innovative research indicates that organization is essential for family stability. Families are more capable of handling change and crisis when there is a degree of continuity and stability through following established routines, home organization, and spending family time together.

This research identifies four family types:

1. *The Unpatterned Family.* This family has never been organized or developed routines. Furthermore, to this family, home organization and routines have no meaning or value.

FOREWORD

2. The Intended Family. This family values organization and routines but never gets around to establishing any. "We should have worship each morning," the family members say, "but there isn't time." They talk about organization but never do anything about it.

3. The Structured Family. Structured families are organized and have many routines in place, but there is no meaning to them. From habit and tradition, the family rigidly follows the patterns established, but the value or meaning is missing.

4. The Rhythmic Family. This family has established many routines and values them. Just having these routines is not important in itself, but the family understands and appreciates their value. For example, giving a child a glass of water is not just a matter of providing a daily quota of liquid. A simple glass of water can become a ritual that encourages the child to feel protected and loved.

Rhythmic families are durable. They can negotiate life's changes with relative comfort because they have created an element of stability through organization and routine. Yara's book can help you become more of a rhythmic family.

I first met Yara through my daughter Carlene Will. Carlene's life is a testimony to the fact that Yara's ideas work. The more sons Carlene produced (at last count there were four!), the more organized she became and the more she could accomplish. Move over, Superwoman! Others, too, have been transformed by the simple techniques Yara teaches, much to the amazement of their family and friends.

Through my own seminars on marriage and parenting, I became vividly aware of the need. I was excited to learn how God was using Yara's talents to help families experience greater stability and cohesiveness through improved home organization.

Yara has spoken to many through her seminars. Now women everywhere can hear her speak through this book—and find much-needed help for Sabbath preparation and establishing organization in the home.

Nancy L. Van Pelt, CHE
Certified Family Life Educator
Certified Home Economist

Acknowledgments

The ideas for this book did not originate in a vacuum. Over the years, so many people have helped and encouraged me, not only as a homemaker but also as a Christian, that I couldn't possibly list them all. However, I do want to specifically thank certain individuals—especially those who have helped me put my ideas into print.

When I started holding seminars, Emilie Barnes unselfishly shared her expertise. She has always encouraged me to put my information in a book.

Charline Davis, a working mother and homemaker, gave me invaluable input. She has been my greatest source of information about the particular needs of the working woman.

Wendy S. A. Innis-Whitehouse, Ph.D., along with my husband, Tom, spent many hours poring over the manuscript and giving valuable grammatical advice.

Julie E. Lombard, whom I lovingly call my guinea pig, was the first to try all my ideas on child rearing, home organization, and Sabbath preparation. Most of all, her prayers have been a source of strength for me.

Guiding me step by step with the writing of this book has been Nancy Van Pelt, herself an often-published author. I am honored that she wrote the foreword to my book.

The advice of my dear friend, Carlene R. Will, has been invaluable to me; she often added ideas that would benefit women in general.

My wonderful husband, Thomas W. Young, M.D., believed that my ideas were worth writing down. He has put as much love, care, support, and work into this book as I have. He did all the initial editing and typing of the manuscript before it was

ACKNOWLEDGMENTS

sent to the publishers. I don't have enough words to thank him.

All my family have been supportive and interested in this project. Their love has encouraged me.

Introduction

Whatever Happened to Sabbath Preparation?

For too many modern Seventh-day Adventist homemakers, the Sabbath has become the day of the rat race rather than the day of rest. As day dies in the west on Friday, many an Adventist woman reclines on the couch trying to recover from the fatigue brought about by the pressures of preparation day. In all of this, one great irony persists: the chaos and frustration come from the desire to have a calm, restful, happy Sabbath day! These women would like to enter into Sabbath rest, but they don't know how to bring it about, how to prepare.

Over the years, I have talked with Adventist women from different parts of the country and from all walks of life. Problems with Sabbath preparation are all too apparent. Those who care about the Sabbath and who try to make it special for themselves and their families are frustrated. Others have stopped trying. For them, the Sabbath has become like any other day of the week. This is too bad. The Sabbath has been something precious that has given Adventists a sense of distinctiveness, but unfortunately, it has lost its meaning for many.

Our lifestyles have changed over the decades. The pace now is much faster, more hectic. Our lives are much more complicated. But our understanding of how to prepare for the holy day has not progressed along with our sophistication. More pressing problems steal our attention.

As Sabbath has become less of a special day, we have grown up with less guidance for how to prepare for it. Role models in this area are few. Whom can we turn to for instruction?

INTRODUCTION

I hope this book will help the beleaguered Adventist home-maker. I'm sure the Lord doesn't want us to miss the blessing we can have from the Sabbath. He knows how desperately we need this important time—especially in such a complicated age! In love, He has given us a weekly reminder of His sovereign power in our lives. Each week, we receive one more opportunity to rededicate our lives to Him, one more opportunity to draw closer to Him, one more opportunity to glorify Him. The Lord intended the Sabbath to be a time of celebration, but too many of us are not having fun anymore!

In this book, I want to emphasize the importance not only of preparing physically for the Sabbath but spiritually as well. Also, this book will cover more than just Sabbath preparation. I will discuss general home maintenance and organization. We will learn how to organize the home from front room to drawers and how to *keep* it organized. These general concepts will support the Sabbath-preparation plan. In fact, the Sabbath becomes the focal point for all homemaking activities. Sabbath preparation will no longer be an activity for Friday; Friday will become the lightest day of the week!

It's not my intent to present hard, inflexible rules on Sabbath preparation, and I certainly don't want this book to be another source of guilt for the struggling Adventist homemaker! Often, our best-laid plans get sidetracked by unforeseen circum-stances. I know this because it happens to me quite often! Still, a good plan is helpful—much more helpful than no plan at all. We need goals, and God has provided Sabbath rest as a useful goal to shoot for. If we aren't successful in reaching our homemaking goals one week, we shouldn't feel like failures. We can try again next week.

Also, I realize that every family is different. Not everything I will share will be of use to all families at all times. Let this book serve as a sourcebook of ideas.

This book brings hope of a better way to prepare for God's holy day. May it be a source of encouragement and instruction, a first step toward regaining the satisfaction and peace many of us have lost through the years.

Chapter 1

Homemaking: What It's All About

As far back as I can remember and throughout my growing years, my parents had a well-worn phrase that they repeated to me often. "Todo lo que te viniere a la mano para hacer," they would tell me in Spanish, "hazlo según tus fuerzas." ("Whatsoever thy hand findeth to do, do it with thy might.") No matter whether the job I faced was large or small, I heard the same words. My brothers and sister heard them too, over and over again. We probably didn't know our ABCs at that time, but we sure could repeat this saying!

That one phrase has much to do with how I now approach life. I found out later that it is a verse from the Bible, from Ecclesiastes 9:10. I always thought it was something my parents had made up! It was their way of telling me to always do my best.

They never told me the second part of the verse: "For there is no work, nor device, nor knowledge, nor wisdom, in the grave, whither thou goest."

What does this mean?

It means that the Lord has given us only one lifetime to live, and mediocrity should not be part of it! I will not have another opportunity to be a daughter, sister, wife, mother, or home-maker. I will not have another opportunity to rear my children and prepare them for the kingdom of God. When we go to the grave, everything stops. Nothing can be redone.

When my parents asked me to do my best, they weren't trying

to get me to do better than someone else. They weren't interested in competition. They simply wanted me to do the most I could, and they considered my age and talents. If a task I completed was not done well but it was the best I could do, it was accepted. If they knew I could do it better, they made me do it over again.

At age sixteen, I was responsible on one occasion for cleaning the whole kitchen. When I finished, I thought I had done a good job and that my mother would be proud of me. When she inspected my work, she called me back into the kitchen. "This kitchen *looks* clean," she said, "but if you study it carefully, there are lots of things that a sixteen-year-old could do better." She pointed out many things I had left undone or failed to clean. "This would have been acceptable for a thirteen-year-old," she continued, "but not for someone your age." She appreciated the work I had done, but she wanted me to be more thorough. With the help, encouragement, and example of my mother, I learned to be thorough. I learned to do my best. I stress this to my children.

As Christians, mediocrity should not be acceptable to us. We must do our work as unto the Lord.

The woman of Proverbs

The Bible gives us an example of a virtuous woman who always did her best. She is often called "the woman of Proverbs," and we can read about her in Proverbs 31:10-31. Preachers like to talk about her in Mother's Day sermons. We rarely notice her at any other time of the year.

I remember once seeing a book titled *How to Become the Woman of Proverbs and Other Impossible Dreams*. The title makes me smile, because I know that is how most of us feel. We say to ourselves, "I am definitely not like the woman of Proverbs."

But the Lord doesn't entice us with impossibilities. He has a goal for us, and by relying on His enabling power, we can reach that goal. There is nothing that our love for Him and His love for us can't accomplish in our lives. We have an advantage that other women who do not love the Lord do not have—the power of the Holy Spirit. "Not by might, nor by power, but by my Spirit, saith the Lord of hosts" (Zechariah 4:6).

It may not be Mother's Day, but let's take time to look more closely at this biblical description of the ideal woman:

Who can find a virtuous woman? for her price is far above rubies.

The heart of her husband doth safely trust in her, so that he shall have no need of spoil.

She will do him good and not evil all the days of her life.

She seeketh wool, and flax, and worketh willingly with her hands.

She is like the merchants' ships; she bringeth her food from afar.

She riseth also while it is yet night, and giveth meat to her household, and a portion to her maidens.

She considereth a field, and buyeth it: with the fruit of her hands she planteth a vineyard.

She girdeth her loins with strength, and strengtheneth her arms.

She perceiveth that her merchandise is good: her candle goeth not out by night.

She layeth her hands to the spindle, and her hands hold the distaff.

She stretcheth out her hand to the poor; yea, she reacheth forth her hands to the needy.

She is not afraid of the snow for her household: for all her household are clothed with scarlet.

She maketh herself coverings of tapestry; her clothing is silk and purple.

Her husband is known in the gates, when he sitteth among the elders of the land.

She maketh fine linen, and selleth it; and delivereth girdles unto the merchant.

Strength and honour are her clothing; and she shall rejoice in time to come.

She openeth her mouth with wisdom; and in her tongue is the law of kindness.

She looketh well to the ways of her household, and eateth not the bread of idleness.

Her children arise up, and call her blessed; her husband

also, and he praiseth her.

Many daughters have done virtuously, but thou excellest them all.

Favour is deceitful, and beauty is vain: but a woman that feareth the Lord, she shall be praised.

Give her of the fruit of her hands; and let her own works praise her in the gates (Proverbs 31:10-31).

You may feel that this description doesn't fit the modern woman. After all, we don't deal with merchant ships too often. I have never held a distaff, and I certainly don't plant vineyards.

Still, God's ideal never changes in principle. His Word is always timely. Maybe the old-fashioned language and the ancient customs make it hard to relate to this description. Here, then, is my modern-language paraphrase of Proverbs 31:10-31.

Who can find a woman with excellent qualities? For she is worth much more than many BMWs.

Her husband has complete confidence in her; he does not lose any sleep.

Throughout their life together, she will do only good things for him.

She does not fear work if it will benefit her family.

She is always looking for a good sale, and occasionally she surprises her family with a new, delicious recipe.

She wakes up early in the morning to get a good start on her busy day, and she helps her family start the day right.

She thinks very carefully about how she spends her money; her financial decisions always bring benefit to all.

She takes time to exercise and look after her health so that she can have the energy she needs to serve her family.

She makes sure that everything she does will help her family. She keeps a flashlight with fresh batteries nearby, just in case.

She makes clothes on her sewing machine and other articles by hand, because she loves to please her family.

She picks out nice things to give to the Salvation Army to help the poor; yes, she is always willing to help others in any way possible.

When the cold months arrive, she pulls out blanket sleepers for her small children to wear and enough blankets so that everyone is warm.

When she sews, she picks good-quality material that will last.

Her husband is successful on the job and in the church, because he has the support of a wise and helpful woman.

Because of the good deals she finds in the stores, she tastefully and beautifully decorates her home without extravagance.

Her self-esteem is strong since she is in control of her household. The future does not scare her because she knows she can face whatever comes.

She does not waste her time in gossip or in speaking nonsense. She speaks to encourage, soothe, and strengthen. Her speech is always clean, and there is kindness in her voice.

She is always doing something constructive and always finds a way to better manage her household.

Her children always say nice things about their mother to others; her husband lavishes her with praise:

"There are many fine women out there, but why have a two-door sedan when you can ride in a Rolls Royce!"

Being popular and beautiful isn't worth much. It is the woman who loves the Lord who is truly valuable.

All one has to do is watch her carefully. The way she works, talks, and acts shows how outstanding she really is.

We can be known as women with excellent qualities if we let the Lord give us the strength to do things with our "might."

Why is good homemaking important?

I want to be like that woman in Proverbs! I feel I share the same concern for the maintenance of my home as she feels for her home. Homemaking is something I want to do well because the well-being of my family depends on it.

There are several reasons to do a good job at home maintenance.

Reason #1: Good homemaking keeps us healthy. If we want

to keep our families healthy, we need to keep the house fresh and clean. Filthy surroundings serve as a breeding ground for disease-producing bacteria. Sunlight and fresh air are also important for the health of the family.

Crawling infants and toddlers in the home often find objects on the floor that we seem to miss—foreign objects that could seriously harm them. Also, mice and some insects are attracted to the crumbs we fail to sweep up or the food we leave out of the cupboard or refrigerator. Insects and mice carry germs and disease.

Our pets can cause unsanitary conditions. They may even cause susceptible people to have allergic reactions. Those who own pets need to pay particular attention to household cleanliness.

Reason #2: Good homemaking provides an example to children. God has given parents of small children an awesome responsibility. During their formative years, children look to us, the parents, as models of social behavior. My children will learn almost everything about housekeeping from me. My little girl will develop the skills for running a home from my instruction.

My boys will also learn from me. Just because they are boys doesn't mean they will only work on car engines. My boys will wash dishes, tubs, and floors. They will also vacuum, cook, and dust. When I was young, my parents often put my older brother in charge of the housecleaning. He would arrange us children in a line at one end of the house. When he gave the order, we moved forward, picking up and replacing anything that was out of place, making everything in our path tidy once again. He did the more difficult tasks, but we worked as a team in every room. My brother cleaned house just as well as my older sister did when she was in charge. And we were finished by noon!

My two sisters-in-law are fortunate. They married men who can clean a house spotlessly, wash any amount of clothes correctly, and cook delicious meals. How did my brothers develop these skills? They learned from my mother.

I don't know how long my sons will be single and living away from home when they are older. But whatever their situation, they will be able to take care of themselves.

When my sister and I got married, housework and cooking never frightened us. Marriage was a new experience for us, but maintaining a home was "old hat." We had learned from the best. We were ready to be homemakers. Now my daughter and my sons are learning not just to do it, but to do it with their might.

Reason #3: Good homemaking fosters pride in the home. I believe we underestimate the feelings our children have about their home. Family members, including children, feel a sense of pride when the home is in good order. Although many forms of pride can be sinful, this type of pride is healthy and promotes a positive image of self and family. I like to think of it as a form of being pleased. The family is pleased with their neat surroundings.

My children always notice when I add something new to the decor of our house. They often say, "I like how this looks." Since they are being reared in a home where neatness and organization are important, they have become used to neat and clean surroundings. My five-year-old twins will actually say, "Let's clean up our bedrooms; they look too messy with all these toys." The desire for a tidy room comes out of their own hearts. When they finish tidying their rooms, they call me. Their faces beam with pride when I enthusiastically compliment them and thank them for their efforts.

My nephew once went with me to visit a friend. He was about eight or nine years old at the time. When we left my friend's house, he immediately asked, "Aunt Yara, why is that lady's house so messy?" I'm glad he didn't say that in front of her! He noticed the state of the home. Children pay attention to much more than we might think. They respond to the condition of their own home with pleasure and pride or with shame.

My mother loves to work in the yard. It's good exercise for her, and she enjoys making the exterior look pretty. Sometimes my father tells her that she overdoes it. She always answers that she likes everything to look nice. One day when my father came home, he said to her, "I'm glad that you make the outside of our house look so attractive. I just came from some homes that looked like they were surrounded by a jungle. It's good to return home and have everything look so nice. Thank you for taking the time."

Reason #4: Our homes reflect our Christianity. The neighbors may have already noticed a difference in us. They may see us on Saturday morning, nicely dressed for church, Bibles in hand. They may see our smiles as we greet them and wave goodbye. They notice our behavior during the week, how we dress, talk, and act. They know that we care about them and are ready to help them in any way possible.

They should also see a difference in the physical part of our home because even this speaks of Christ.

In a parking lot one day, I noticed a bumper sticker that asked: "Is your life a message or a mess?" At first I chuckled, but then I thought about my life. "Am I a message for God, or am I a mess?" We should tell others what Christ has done for us; this is good and important. But often, the real message comes from the way we live, not the words we say. God wants to use our lives to show His power.

I am amazed at how often a messy home reflects the personal turmoil and confusion of the caretaker. Of course, any home may be messy every now and then, but when a home is messy all the time, it's as if the confusion on the outside reflects the confusion on the inside. On the other hand, an orderly home speaks strongly of an orderly life, a life controlled by the power of God. I realize that this observation is not accurate 100 percent of the time, but I certainly believe there is a connection. What do others who are not Christians think of our belief in God when they see our messy homes?

As the child's song reminds us, we are "a sermon in shoes." No sermon speaks louder than our lifestyle, and lifestyle includes the way we keep our homes. If we want our lives to be a message and not a mess, we must pay attention to 1 Corinthians 14:40: "Let all things be done decently and in order."

How the Sabbath became important to me

Over the years, the Sabbath has been the focal point of all my home-maintenance activities. My understanding of the connection between housekeeping and the role of the Sabbath has evolved over the years as my concept of the Sabbath and its importance to me has changed.

When I was a teenager, growing up in my parents' home,

Sabbath was a time to see my friends and enjoy being with them. Many of my social activities at that time revolved around the church and its activities. During the week, I attended a public school in which I didn't have too many friends, so I looked forward to the Sabbath and all the activities of that day. I learned to love the church and what it had to offer me.

While in college, Sabbath became much more to me than simply a social time. Because of the pressure of classes, assignments, and examinations, the Sabbath became important to me for physical and mental rest.

After college, when I became both a married and a working woman, my Sabbath emphasis changed again. There was still the important social aspect, and, yes, the Sabbath was still important to me for physical and mental rest. But I also had a desire to make the Sabbath meaningful for our new home. From our first Sabbath as Mr. and Mrs. Young, I wanted to establish traditions that would be meaningful to us as a married couple, just as those of my childhood home were meaningful to me. I have noticed that the customs we establish during the first weeks of marriage often set the tone for the rest of our married lives. I discuss some of these traditions in chapter 8 of this book.

I wanted my husband, Tom, to see a marked difference in our home on Fridays compared with any other weekday. I wanted him to feel special as he entered our tiny apartment. A medical student's life is mentally taxing, so I wanted to help him relax and feel excited about coming home to receive the Sabbath with his bride. I wanted his home to be a place where he could be rejuvenated before the onslaught of studies came around again. Having a tidy home helped us relax and anticipate the Sabbath with joy.

When I had my first child, my Sabbath emphasis changed once again. Now I wanted to do everything I could to cause our children to love the Sabbath. This is still my goal and will be until our children leave home. I want them to look forward to the Sabbath every week. As they become teenagers, I will try to emphasize even more the joy of this special day.

We need a goal

Not all of us were born with a scrub brush in one hand and

a container of cleanser in the other. Most of us don't relish the thought of cleaning and keeping up with the home. This is normal. There is nothing wrong with us if we feel less than enthusiastic about housework. So we must come up with a plan that will help us. If we don't, we will clean only in a crisis.

What happens when Mother-in-Law calls and tells us that she will pay us a visit this coming weekend? Do we run around madly, cleaning as fast as we can? What about that friend we so admired from school days who calls to say she will be passing through? Do we hit the house like a tornado, trying to get ready for her visit?

Wouldn't it be nice to be ready at *any* time? You bet!

I know it's not possible to be ready anytime *all* of the time. Emergencies will sometimes ruin our plans, no matter how good they are. Still, getting ready for surprise guests might not be as hard as it could be if we carefully follow a plan most of the time.

In order to be ready anytime, we need a goal and a plan to allow us to reach it. I have a goal that helps me keep my house clean throughout the week and be ready for the Sabbath.

My goal is *to have my home at the peak of cleanliness by Friday morning.*

This objective not only helps me prepare the physical part of the house for the Sabbath but also gives me an opportunity to enhance my spiritual growth. Just think how clear our minds can be when we are ready for Sabbath so early! We can meditate, pray, and ask the Holy Spirit to give us perceptive minds and hearts for what we will hear and read during those wonderful Sabbath hours.

This goal also gives me time to teach my children about positive Sabbath attitudes. I have the time to talk, explain, and answer their questions. It gives me time to enhance the meaning and beauty of the Sabbath for my family. There are other benefits too.

Readiness for unexpected company

One Friday evening while the family was eating supper, the telephone rang. The brother of a good friend was driving from California to Virginia. He and a friend were driving through eastern Nebraska. Not wanting to travel on the Sabbath, they phoned to see if they could spend Friday night, Saturday, and Saturday evening with us.

Such a request would have sent a lot of people into a tailspin! We weren't expecting them. We did not even know they were in the area. But following my goal of having the house clean by Friday morning now made it possible for me to respond calmly. Without a thought, I told them that we would be happy to have them stay with us and that I was glad they had thought of us.

I didn't race around the house, trying to make it ready for our guests. We continued eating as if nothing had happened. We made only one change. We put our sons to sleep in our bedroom so that our guests could sleep in the boys' room. The boys' room was already spotlessly clean, and both beds had freshly laundered bedding. When our friends arrived, they apologized for the inconvenience they had given us. The truth was that they had been no inconvenience whatsoever. We thoroughly enjoyed our Sabbath together.

Why was I so relaxed and prepared? It was because I met my goal that week.

The chances for unexpected company are higher on the weekends than during the week. Should Aunt Matilda call Friday morning to say she will arrive Friday by sunset, there is no need to fret or frown if we have been working carefully toward the goal. Even if the house were not completely "spotless" at the time of her call, there wouldn't be that much of a problem. There would be no mountain of laundry on the floor, no stack of dirty dishes to wash, no unmade beds—we would be ready or almost ready!

Another benefit to having everything done by Friday morning is that I don't have to spend Sundays doing major housework. We plan activities for the family. Weekends are very special for us, and I don't want washing, mopping, or any other major task to get in the way of enjoying my husband and children. Wouldn't a free Sunday be nice?

So what are we waiting for?

In the rest of this book, I will share the specifics—the "nuts and bolts"—that go into making this goal a reality. Our situations may differ, but I believe everyone who needs help with home organization and Sabbath preparation can find helpful ideas in this book. Most of all, it is my prayer that these ideas may enhance your life as a Christian and your walk with the Lord Jesus Christ!

May all that we do as homemakers be done for the honor and glory of God and for the benefit of our families!

Chapter 2

The Night Before Is the Key to the Next Day

The most important home-organization idea in this book can be stated simply in ten words: *The night before is the key to the next day.* This idea will make the difference between success and failure. All that you will read in the rest of this book will be effective largely to the degree that you heed this concept religiously.

What does this mean—The night before is the key to the next day? It means that if we tidy up the house in the evening before going to bed, then maintaining the home will be simple. We will be "ahead of the game." If we fail to tidy up the house in the evening before going to bed, then we will have a more difficult time. We will be "behind the eight ball."

So what can we do in the evenings? First, let me explain how I get my seven-year-old and my twin five-year-olds ready for bed. Putting young children to bed can wear down even the most patient homemaker.

Picking up and organizing the toys

Around four-thirty in the afternoon, my children pick up all their toys and anything else they have left out during the day. I make sure that all toys are gathered from the family room, the bedrooms, and everywhere else in the house. While they are picking up their toys, I also do some tidying up. I put away any books or papers that I left out. I also start making everything look nice again, fluffing pillows and straightening articles of furniture. During this whole time I keep an eye on the children to make sure they are putting their toys in the right places.

I have a place for all the toys, and the children know where everything goes. I expect them to put everything in its proper place and not to throw toys in any old nook and cranny. All must be in order.

I favor toy shelves over toy chests. It is impossible to keep a toy chest organized, and it's almost impossible to find small toys among the larger ones. In the process of finding one small toy, kids will often empty out the whole chest. Toys are much easier to find on toy shelves.

My toy shelves consist of a large metal shelf case with five shelves and a few plastic dishpans. The dishpans are the same color, and each stores a different type of toy. One container has Mr. Potato Heads, another is filled with Matchbox cars, another contains larger cars, another has Legos, another has Bible characters, another has wooden blocks, etc. My children don't throw Matchbox cars in the large car container, and they don't throw Legos in the wooden block container.

A friend was amazed one day at how carefully my children put their toys away. She would ask them where each toy should be placed, and they would tell her.

Having separate containers for each toy makes it easy for the kids to use their toys without making a large mess. For instance, if they want to play with Legos, they pull out the Lego pan, leaving the other toys undisturbed. When they are finished, they put the Legos back in the pan and place it on the shelf without much fuss. I even have a miscellaneous dishpan for odds and ends—magnifying glass, binoculars, Gumby. Believe it or not, my kids never try to put toys in the miscellaneous pan that don't belong there.

Larger toys that do not fit in dishpans are stored in a corner close to the shelves. I also have smaller toy shelves with small plastic baskets in each of the children's rooms. These contain cassette tapes, paper, crayons, scissors, marking pens, and other small items. The children also have a case for all their books, and they know where each book belongs.

Plastic dishpans and baskets are not expensive. You can find them in any discount store. This system keeps items organized, makes it easy to put toys away, and makes it easy to take out toys that are needed. I have also set up one central toy and play area. This makes cleaning the house much easier.

The "four-thirty pickup" is not too difficult because everyone knows where every toy belongs.

Bathtime

After we have tidied up the whole house, the children get ready for their baths. They go to their rooms and undress themselves. They put all their dirty clothing in their hampers. That's the first chore I taught my oldest son when he started walking. He now puts all his clothes in the hamper every day. As a matter of fact, he took it upon himself to teach the twins to put their clothes in the hamper!

I believe every room should have a clothes hamper. This keeps us from having to pick up clothes from the floor. Also, if there is a hamper in each room, it's easy to do the wash for each individual person as the need arises.

When the children were younger, I would bathe all three at the same time. Now, I bathe the twins one at a time, and my oldest son bathes himself. Since my children are now older and since they have played heartily all day, I don't make their baths another playtime. I shampoo each child's hair, soap down his body and face, rinse him thoroughly, and then take him out of the tub. The next child comes into the tub as the clean one puts on pajamas.

When the baths are done, I close the shower curtain and hang up the towels. I give a "once over" to the commode and sink with disinfectant spray, and then I leave. One could come into the bathroom at that point and never know that I had just given the kids a bath. I don't have to come back to clean up the bathroom.

Evening activities

I try to slow the kids down after their baths. They read books, color, or play a quiet game. Meanwhile, I put supper together quickly. We have light suppers. My children eat between 5:00

and 5:30 p.m. Daddy is not always home for supper. A doctor's hours are not fixed, so most weekdays we don't wait for him. On Friday, he does his best to be home before 6:00 p.m., and he is usually successful.

After supper, we brush teeth and have worship. After worship, Daddy is usually home. The kids play and often "roughhouse" with him before going to bed. Right before bed they use the bathroom, and I take a cup of water to their night stands.

The twins go to bed between 7:00 and 7:15 p.m. While they are in bed, I go through their rooms and tidy up anything that was too difficult for them to do. If I find something they forgot to do, I get them out of bed and have them do it. Then Tom and I kiss them good night and give them a final hug. When I close their doors, I leave behind neat and orderly rooms. The only things that are messy are their beds. Our oldest boy goes to bed at 8:00 p.m. and, until bedtime, he plays quietly or shares with Daddy all that he did at school that day.

After the twins are in bed, Tom and I have supper (unless he came home early enough to have supper with the children). When I clear the table, I set it once again for breakfast. We use the rest of the evening doing what we want (such as writing this book).

Before I retire for the night, I think about what needs to be done for the next day. I might put some beans in water to soak through the night. Or I may put beans in the crock-pot to cook on low for tomorrow's lunch or dinner. I may put whole grains in the crock-pot for tomorrow's cereal. I may put a load of clothes in the washing machine. Or I may sort some clothes. Whatever it is, I try to see what I can do that evening to make tomorrow easier. The last thing I do before going to bed is turn on the dishwasher.

As we prepare for bed, we hang up the garments that need to be hung. Our dirty clothes go in our hamper, and the shoes go in the shoe rack in the closet. When we go to bed, our room is tidy and in order. If someone were to come to our house at 3:00 a.m., he would find only four messy beds, and that is only because we would be sleeping in them!

The importance of "the night before"

My routine is simply an example of one way to organize the

evening hours. Because your circumstances will vary from mine, you need to develop a routine that will be useful for your family. Nevertheless, my "take home" message remains the same: maintaining the house the following day will be less of a burden if you remember to tidy up the night before.

It's a nice feeling to go to bed and know that the whole house is tidy. You can have that feeling daily. Recently, at one of my home-organization seminars, a woman commented, "Ever since your seminar I can't think of going to sleep without tidying up. It has made such a difference." Another said, "I can use all your ideas, but if I don't pick up the night before, none of the other ideas fall into place."

One woman failed to see the need to clean up the night before. "I know that picking up the night before is good, but if I don't feel like doing it, I just realize that the dishes in the sink will still be there the next day when I get up, so I don't worry."

It's true that you can put off dealing with the mess until the following morning, but if you do, there will be less time the next day to do what needs to be done. The time you spend catching up cuts into quality time for the family and for yourself. It's hard to make changes, I know, but sometimes changes bring good results and make life easier.

Tidying up the night before will make all the difference in the world the next day. Once I had gone for about three weeks without doing a major cleanup when I had some guests over to my house. None of them would have ever thought my house was dirty. I had kept up by just tidying up the night before. After you read chapter 4, it will be apparent what kind of difference picking up the night before can make.

What if there is an emergency?

Sometimes, in spite of our best intentions, things happen to prevent us from tidying up the house in the evening. Junior may need help typing a term paper that is due the next day. Your daughter may need help with the finishing touches on the dress she is making for the banquet the next day. What, then, if we can't tidy up the evening before?

We can do one of two things. We can wake up early the next morning and tidy up the house before we start our daily routine.

Or we can forget about it. At times, when I don't put things away the night before, I don't pay much attention to the mess the next day. When evening rolls around and it is once again time to "tidy up," I will pick up then.

Still, I am a believer in "the night before." I can't overemphasize it: *The night before is the key to the next day.*

Chapter 3

Starting the Day Right

When Monday morning rolls around again and a brand new week has started, I begin working toward my weekly goal: to have my house in tiptop condition for the Sabbath. I wake up at 5:00 a.m. It isn't even light yet. Why so early? Because I want to start the day right. I want to start it with the Lord.

This devotional time with God is the most important aspect of my life as a Christian homemaker. It is this early-morning experience with Him that reminds me what the important priorities in my life are. I gain direction and purpose for my life during that time. If we want to do all for the glory of God, we must daily seek Him first. If we depend on our own strength and efforts, we may get by, but we will miss out on His blessing. We may do good things, but we will not allow the Lord to show us the best things. We may fail to discern the Lord's guidance for us.

For some, five o'clock in the morning may not be the best time to look for spiritual guidance. It's hard to commune with God if our eyes are closed—in sleep, not in prayer. Five o'clock in the morning happens to be the best time for me.

I had always heard that the early morning was the best time for devotions. At one time, I tried to prove those words wrong. I had devotions at just about every hour of the day *except* for the morning. I tried to have my devotions while my children napped, but I found out quickly that they were not the only ones napping. I would join them every time. I tried the evening. I soon

33

found out that I ended up doing many other things before I even thought of devotions. I tried to have my devotional time while the children were awake, but settling arguments, tying shoes, cleaning noses, and comforting little hurts do not mix with personal quiet time. So with a strong feeling of defeat, I tried those unearthly morning hours. Believe it or not, they worked for me. When I set aside those first moments of the day, I know I will take the time to commune with God. Otherwise, I've found I will not get around to having my devotions.

The early morning works for me, but I realize that this time may not be suitable for everyone. We all face different demands on our time, and we should adjust our devotional schedules accordingly. Also, some may not function well at all in the early morning. The most important thing is to have a devotional experience, so if early morning isn't the right time for you, find a time that is!

Four reasons devotional time is important

1. Devotions help us develop a meaningful relationship with God. In order to have a close relationship with the Lord and to know His will for my life, I must spend time with Him.

It works like this. You know me just a little bit from reading this book, but I probably know nothing about you. Now, if I start calling you on the telephone and talking to you, we'll get to know each other somewhat. Furthermore, if I start sending you notes, and we start setting dates to get together, we would get to know each other better. During this time, our relationship will go through different levels—from a superficial knowledge to truly knowing each other. I will come to know what you like and what you don't like. I will learn what brings you joy and what brings you sadness. I will know your aspirations and your fears. When you call me on the phone, I will recognize your voice immediately. As our friendship grows, I will know that I can call on you for help, support, wisdom, a listening ear, or a shoulder to cry on. Most important, I will learn to love you. I have friends right now with whom I share this type of relationship. It didn't happen overnight; it took time to forge this kind of bond.

That is how it can be with God and us. When we take time to be with Him, we will truly get to know Him. We will find out what

He wants from us. We will know what glorifies Him and what does not. We will know what He has planned for our lives. We will learn to trust and love Him.

What do we do when we love someone? We serve them. Let me give an example of this kind of loving service. My husband is extremely supportive of me in all that I do. He has worked on this book as much as I have. He helps me in every aspect when I prepare for a seminar. He goes to as many seminars and workshops as his schedule permits. For every church activity I plan, he is right there, helping to make it a success. Why does he do this? The answer is *love*. His support is one strong way that he tells me he loves me.

He gets the same response from me. The love I have for him motivates me to please and "serve" him. My marriage to him has meant moving from the West Coast to the East Coast, far from the family I love. Yet, knowing how important his professional growth is to him and knowing that he does not spare anything for my happiness, how could I not willingly follow him anywhere? Knowing what God has done for us and what He will continue to do for us, we can only love Him in response. That is what it means to have a meaningful relationship with God.

2. Devotions help us to become godly women. To become like God should be our main goal in life. A change from our selfish, human ways to God's ways can happen in our lives as we seek Him daily through our devotions. Such a change is not possible in our own strength, but through the Holy Spirit, what was once impossible now becomes possible.

As we study the life of Jesus, how He responded to people and situations, we learn how to be godly. Have you noticed how easily we are influenced by those we admire and spend time with? Each of my close friends has had an influence on me. Fortunately, they have been women who truly love the Lord, so their influence on me has been positive.

As we come to know our friends better, we may find ourselves liking some of the things they like, seeing things the way they do, and learning from them. The same can happen as a result of our friendship with Jesus. Through the Scriptures, we see how Jesus treated the woman at the well. We see how He treated the woman caught in adultery. We see Him as the Good

Samaritan. We see His responses to Pontius Pilate and to those who struck Him and spat on His face during His trial. We see Him lovingly feed the multitude. He loved and cared for everyone. His dependence on His Father was complete. We see the ultimate in love from Him as He died to save us. And we will find ourselves reflecting His attitudes in our own lives.

No desire in our hearts should be greater than to be like Him, to have our hearts changed, and to have Him sanctify us. Our daily devotional experience will allow these desires to be fulfilled.

3. *Devotions allow us to receive power from above.* Because of the stress and difficulty of life and because of our human natures, we often fall short of what God expects of us. In our own strength, we are unable to live as we desire to live. We want to serve the Lord. We want to be like Him. We want others to see Him in us. We want to treat everyone as brothers and sisters. We want to be godly. We have great expectations. But of ourselves we cannot do any of these things. We need power from above to become the persons we should be. Only His power can bring about a new nature and cause our attitudes to become holy attitudes. We are told to ask for this power. The Lord does not walk into our lives without us giving Him permission. He patiently waits for us to ask for Him and His power. Our devotions give us the time and opportunity to do this.

4. *Devotions help us clarify our priorities in life.* When we spend time with the Lord daily, we find out what is important to Him. The Holy Spirit leads us to realize that those things should also be important to us. These priorities help us see all of life as sacred. For life to run smoothly, we first must seek the Lord daily and have a relationship with Him. Only then will the responsibilities of wife, mother, career, and homemaker fall into their rightful places. What once seemed so important will not seem important anymore. Other items that were not important now hold great importance. Things will be brought into focus. Love, forgiveness, kindness, and understanding will gain true meaning.

What may happen when we start

So suppose we now start having devotions. Will all these good results start happening immediately? Will we become the godly, Spirit-filled persons we desire to be? Will the "impossible" dream come true? All these things will happen—but not immediately. Before devotions make a positive difference, we may experience some negative times. Several women have told me, "As soon as I started devotions, my days started to go terribly. I did better without a devotional time."

There is a logical explanation for this horrible turn of events. Satan, our enemy, the prince of darkness, the liar, and the deceiver, wants us to get discouraged. He would like to deceive us into thinking that a life far away from Christ is better than one close to Him!

Before we begin our devotional time, he has us where he wants us. Our characters are not becoming more like Christ's, since we don't really know Him. We don't possess the power and strength that come from the Holy Spirit to change our lives. Going to church means nothing unless we love the One we go to church to worship. Satan knows this very well. His greatest desire is for us to be fooled into thinking that we are living like Jesus when we are not.

But when we start working on a relationship with God, Satan gets scared. "This woman is putting forth an effort to start her day with God," he says. "I'm afraid she'll get to know Him. I'd better ruin her efforts." So Satan plans ways to discourage us about getting to know God. He will distract us during our devotional time with many interruptions. Or he will make us feel that our day goes better without God. Satan knows that the more we know the Lord and the greater the amount of His power that we have, the less control he has over us. He wants to have full control because he wants to destroy us.

Several years ago, I led a women's Bible-study group through a book on prayer. Before reading this book, I was not pleased with my prayer life. After five minutes of praying, I couldn't think of anything else to pray about! But as I read this book, I learned what prayer was about and how to pray. I was thrilled! During my early-morning devotional time, when I tried to put into practice what I learned, all of a sudden my children began to wake up earlier, interrupting my prayer time. They decided that five-thirty in the morning was a perfect time to cry and demand attention. This happened day after day right at my prayer time. Before this, the kids never woke up at five-thirty; they always slept until six-thirty. It dawned on me that Satan was trying to disrupt my prayer life. I made arrangements with my husband to tend to the children as I continued praying.

For two weeks the children continued to wake up at five-thirty each morning. I continued on my knees, and my husband would care for the kids. After those two weeks, they never woke up at five-thirty again. My prayer life has flourished. Five minutes used to be my maximum praying time; now thirty minutes is not enough.

When we start our devotional life and everything goes wrong, we should rejoice! This tells us that Satan has good reason to worry. We are heading down the right road. So let's not allow Satan to discourage us. Let's continue our devotions regardless of the circumstances. As our relationship with the Lord is strengthened, Satan will have less power over us.

In the beginning, we won't feel like having devotions. I know this from personal experience. But if we let that feeling take over, we will never have devotions. These feelings must not weaken our resolve. We should have devotions, not because *we* want to, but because *God* wants us to have them. Do we need a better motivation? As we get to know Him better, we will look forward to spending time with Him daily.

Pick a special place and time

Have a set time for devotions. If we don't include this time in our schedules, we will probably never get around to doing it. Pick a special place. A nice well-lighted corner with a chair is helpful, but make sure the chair is not too soft. We don't want to fall asleep. This special place will put us in a worshipful frame of mind. Keep the devotional materials nearby in a shelf or basket.

I spend about an hour in my devotional time each day. For me, this is plenty of time. For some, that may be too long. For others, it may not be long enough. I feel that the length of time is not important. Our devotions should be long enough for us to grow spiritually but not so long that they become boring.

The worship basket

My good friend, Carlene Will, gave me an excellent idea for a "worship basket." That's what she called a wicker basket in which she kept her devotional materials. Carlene and I went shopping for my basket, and after four hours in the mall, we finally found the perfect one. We then decorated the basket and handle with ribbon and lace.

I keep my Bible, my Sabbath School quarterly, one or more devotional books, a prayer notebook, and a small bag with markers, pens, and pencils in this basket. Everything I need is at my fingertips in an organized and attractive manner. The basket made my devotional experience even more fun. The worship basket would make a good gift for a friend. Even my husband has a worship basket, although I didn't put lace or anything frilly around it! His basket is deep and sturdy, and he keeps all his devotional materials in it.

Getting started

Women frequently ask me, "How do I start my devotions? What do I read? The Bible makes me fall asleep. How did you start?"

I don't have all the answers, but I can share what I have done. Initially, I picked books written especially for women and their spiritual needs. Several such books are in print about how to become a woman of God, how to use our special talents for God's glory, how special a woman who loves the Lord can be. I read many of these books. We must pick books that meet our needs and interests. Don't read something that induces sleep.

Later I read books about salvation and Christian living. At that point, I began feeling guilty about not reading the Bible. I knew the importance of reading the Bible, but I had no desire. I also have a husband who is extremely knowledgeable in the Scriptures. Here I was, a minister's daughter, yet I could not boast of any significant scriptural knowledge. Oh, sure, I knew all the Bible stories, but could I defend my faith with the holy Book? I couldn't. I decided to learn my Bible a little better.

I didn't go directly to the Bible at first. Instead, I went to Arthur Maxwell's ten-volume *Bible Story* set. This set starts in Genesis and goes to Revelation. In essence, I read a large outline of the Bible. My husband noticed that I had become excited about my devotions. He asked what I was reading. I was too embarrassed to tell him directly. Instead, I told him I was reading a good book that made the Bible clear to me. He insisted on knowing what the book was; maybe he would be interested in it. Now I was really embarrassed! I told him what I was reading. He said, "As long as you are learning and growing, that's fine."

After I finished those ten volumes, I bought books that explained certain portions of the Bible. Then I started reading the short books of the Bible. The last eleven books of the Old Testament are short. There are also several books in the New Testament with six chapters or less.

Now I am studying the Bible, and I love it. I truly enjoy it. Little by little, I am becoming more knowledgeable in the Scriptures.

Studying the Sabbath School lesson daily is also a good way to start. Remember, first start with materials that are immediately helpful, perhaps even a book on self-esteem, home organization, marriage, or simple principles of how to become a Christian. Once those initial needs are met, you will grow spiritually and develop an appetite for the stronger "meat" of the Bible.

Prayer

Some of us use prayer as sailors use life preservers. We pray only when the problems seem insurmountable. Prayer should be much more than that. Even the Saviour, all-powerful and all-knowing as He was, took time to pray regularly. "He withdrew himself into the wilderness, and prayed" (Luke 5:16). "And in the morning, rising up a great while before day, he went out, and departed into a solitary place, and there prayed" (Mark 1:35).

If Jesus, as perfect and as sinless as He is, needed the power that comes from prayer, how much more do we need to pray. We need to pray not only for ourselves but also for others. The Lord wants us to pray for each other.

I don't intend to write a whole chapter on prayer, but I feel that prayer is a very important part of our devotional experience. By praying, we lay all our burdens, big or small, on God's shoulders. We plead for Him to help us become more like Him. We daily die to self and ask Him to live for us. We ask for complete forgiveness for our sins and then thank Him for that forgiveness. We ask Him for strength to meet the pressures of the day.

Notice that I haven't mentioned using prayer to ask God for what we want out of life—that house, that car, that dress, that dining-room set. Prayer is not a blank check for our materialistic desires. I am not saying that the Lord will not give us those things. We receive them from the proper use of the money and other means with which He has entrusted us. God, however, has not promised us riches here in this world. He has promised to give us what we need. And if we seek the kingdom of God first, other blessings will follow.

In her book *Talking With God* (Zondervan, 1985), Glaphre Gilliland shares the divine pattern for prayer. It is the pattern that Jesus taught us in the Sermon on the Mount. It is a pattern I learned to use, and it has made all the difference in my prayer life.

"Our Father which art in heaven." When we begin to pray, we need to recognize God's presence with us. Until we recognize this presence, prayer loses its meaning.

"Hallowed be thy name." Here, we worship God. We recognize that He is holy, good, pure, powerful, and full of majesty. We are reminded of the kind of God who owns us.

"Thy kingdom come. Thy will be done in earth, as it is in heaven." This part of our prayer reminds us that we are not in control. We recognize God's leading. We cannot tell Him what to do about our situation. This part of the prayer shows that we trust fully in His will for our lives.

"Give us this day our daily bread." After we have submitted to God and His will for our lives, we can then ask Him to supply our needs.

"And forgive us our debts, as we forgive our debtors." If our prayers are going to be answered, we must do two things. First, we must ask for and receive God's forgiveness. Second, we must forgive others. In this part of the prayer, we should search our hearts and make sure these conditions are met.

"And lead us not into temptation, but deliver us from evil." We must pray this prayer long *before* we are faced with temptation. The closer we get to the Lord, the more subtle Satan becomes with his temptations. When we realize how much we need God's

deliverance in our lives, we will know how often to pray that prayer.

"For thine is the kingdom, and the power, and the glory, for ever." Our prayer should end much like it started. We must declare that the glory belongs to God and God alone.

"Amen." We end our prayer saying, "You are in charge. I believe You will take care of everything. It is all Yours!"

This pattern of prayer will allow us to communicate more effectively with God.

Prayer organization

Finally, I would like to share how I organize my prayers. It may seem odd to organize something as personal as prayer, but I have found it very helpful. Organizing prayer enables me to give each of my prayer requests enough time.

My friend Emilie Barnes is an expert on Christian time management. Emilie presents the idea of prayer organization in her books and seminars. I have tailored many of her ideas to my needs. Here they are.

Buy a three-ring binder. Any size will do. Mine is seven inches by ten inches. Buy seven dividers and at least a hundred sheets of paper. Divide the notebook into seven equal sections, each division representing a day of the week. In each section I record: (1) a specific category of items to pray for on that day, (2) specific prayer requests related to each category, and (3) specific answers to prayer from the Lord. I also record special insights during my Bible study that I might want to review at a later time.

These are my prayer categories for each day.

Sunday: My pastor and his family, my church leaders, our country and its leaders, missionaries.

Monday: Our children, my family, my husband's family.

Tuesday: My friends and their requests.

Wednesday: Personal items, including my seminars and book, my church responsibilities.

Thursday: My husband and his activities, his prayer requests.

Friday: I ask for the Holy Spirit to mold my character, to help our family be what He wants us to be.

Sabbath: I use this section for Sabbath School lesson and sermon notes and for jotting down prayer requests from others.

Of course, I pray for my husband and children every day, but not in the thorough way that I do on the days especially devoted to them. My prayer organization ensures that I don't forget anyone and that I'm not rushed at prayer time.

It is now Monday morning, and I have started my day. Most important, I have started my day right. "Seek ye first the kingdom of God, and his righteousness; and all these things shall be added unto you" (Matthew 6:33).

Chapter 4

Steps to Sabbath Preparation— Starting With Monday

The previous three chapters have dealt with the "basics." Now we're ready to grapple with the nuts and bolts of this matter of Sabbath preparation. Come walk with me through the rest of my week, and you will see how it's possible for Friday to become the easiest day of the week. I'll also be discussing several other important topics on the way.

I have noticed that the idea of Friday as the lightest workday of the week intrigues many women. "How do you do *that*?" is written all over the faces of some. Others shake their heads as if to say "No way." The idea is too far-fetched. I can tell that many of these women have tried to make Friday less burdensome, but in vain. When I cover this topic in my seminar, everyone sits up straight, prepared to take down every word. I suppose they expect a simple, secret formula, expressed in a single sentence or two. But in reality it takes careful planning throughout the whole week in order for Friday to be the lightest day.

Before I go on, here are a few words for the faint of heart. What follows may seem like a lot to do and a lot to think about, but please keep an open mind until you have looked at my routine from start to finish. Many who have attended my seminars initially thought my routine was too difficult for them to follow, but now their Fridays are lighter than any other day. Remember, too, that it's all right to crawl before you walk or run. Master the basics, and then add the fine points as you go along.

Monday morning—rise and shine!

It is 6:00 a.m. I have just finished having my devotions, and now I'm ready to start the day—the first workday of the week.

First I wake my husband so that he can go running. As soon as he gets up, I immediately make our bed. The bedspread now looks nice, and the throw pillows are all in place. Now, what else do I need to do in my bedroom to have it ready for the day? Nothing! Everything was done the night before. I went to bed in a neat, tidy room, remember? Now all I have to do is make the bed!

Do you know how awful it is to wake up in a messy room? The sight of pants thrown in one corner; dirty clothes lying all around; a mountain of shoes in the middle of the room; stockings hanging over the chair; a dresser cluttered with purses, books, and scarves! It's enough to make us want to throw the blankets over our heads and never get up. We feel tired before we have even started; we don't even want to start. Am I glad I picked up the night before!

I have made the bed, and now the whole room is ready for the day. I walk out of the room, knowing that I won't have to come back to clean it. Everything is in its place.

Now I go to the kitchen to prepare breakfast. What do I see? The table is set. The bowls, flatware, glasses, and napkins are all in place. I set the table the night before, remember? Of course, to do that, I needed to know what I would serve for breakfast the next morning.

Breakfast tips

In a talk I gave about organizational skills to an audience of both men and women, I asked, "How many of you are in the cold-cereal rut?" Most of the men nodded their heads emphatically in the affirmative. The women just smiled. The cold-cereal rut exists nationwide. If you would like to try something different for breakfast, here are a few ideas.

I know the night before what I will serve for breakfast just by knowing what day it will be. On Sunday night I will put out bowls because Monday morning I will serve hot cereal. It will be

Cream of Wheat, cooked oats, or whole grains that are left cooking overnight in the crock-pot.

Monday night, I will set the table with plates because Tuesday I will serve wheat waffles, pancakes, or French toast.

Tuesday night, I will use bowls again because Wednesday I will serve another type of hot cereal.

Wednesday night, I will use plates because Thursday I will serve some type of egg or tofu dish.

Thursday and Friday nights, I will set the table with bowls because Friday and Sabbath mornings I serve cold cereal.

Sunday mornings, I serve my "fancy breakfast." I go all out so that it ends up being more like a Sunday brunch. The whole family looks forward to this breakfast. I try to prepare potatoes in different ways. One week I may bake them; other weeks I may boil or fry them. I usually sauté mushrooms, because my husband *loves* mushrooms. I also serve broccoli and some type of protein dish.

Toast, juice, and fruit are a part of every breakfast.

Breakfast can become an enjoyable meal! It should be the most important meal of the day. Even with the time constraints of our busy lives, it takes only a little planning and preparation the night before to make breakfast enjoyable.

A homemaker who attended one of my seminars called me a week later to tell me about breakfast. "Breakfast is now a *wonderful* meal," she said. Her family couldn't believe the change. They had had blueberry muffins that morning for breakfast! The previous day, she had made orange bread. The following day, they were going to have a rice casserole. Her breakfast menu used to be cold cereal, day after day, and now look at the creative difference. You don't have to make breakfasts as elaborate as this, but neither do you have to stay in the cold-cereal rut. I try to please everyone in my family by giving each person his favorite dish on one morning during the week. My children love waffles, so Tuesday is waffle day. My husband enjoys hot cereal, so Monday and Wednesday are his days.

One word of warning about breakfast. Don't try to make the breakfast nook into a restaurant, and don't offer each family member a menu! You shouldn't break your back every day trying to please each person with his favorite dish. Your kitchen isn't a smorgasbord, and you aren't a waitress. The family should work together, functioning in an organized manner.

Many women tell me it is easier for them to make whatever each individual family member wants because then there are no hassles. They say their children complain and cry when they don't get what they want.

What are we really telling our children by giving in to such demands? Shouldn't we teach them, instead, how to eat nutritiously? If we take the time to train our families properly, they will enjoy good food, and there will be no hassles!

Preparing for breakfast

Now, let's get back to our walk through Monday morning. I finish my breakfast preparations. I take out of the refrigerator the orange juice that I prepared from concentrate the night before. I put out the fruit and whatever else I need for the meal.

I awaken my oldest son at six-thirty. He prays, and then we make the bed together. Now that his bed is made, what else do I need to do? *Nothing!* Everything is already clean and tidy from the night before. Now I awaken the twins and go through the same process with them. Soon, the bedrooms are ready for the day.

Now, through our mind's eye, let's walk through the house and see what condition it is in. We pass by the master bedroom; it is tidy and clean. We pass by the children's rooms; they are tidy and clean. We go to the living room, the dining room, the family room, and the bathrooms. Every room is clean and tidy, *and it is not even seven o'clock in the morning yet!*

What fantastic magic trick did I perform? What army of maids came through the house at night? What did I have to do to have the house in such a condition so early in the morning? I made four beds. That's all.

What was the key? The night before is the answer.

I go back to the kitchen and make the last breakfast preparations. At seven o'clock, the family sits down at the table to have breakfast.

Here is how I dealt with breakfast when my children were still very young. Many might not agree with the following idea, but at least it is something to think about. Before the children were two years old, I fed them breakfast before my husband and I had our breakfast. It was easier for us that way. I was able to enjoy my husband during the meal without much interruption. I didn't have to get up constantly to wipe up messes or to comfort crying children. My husband and I could truly enjoy the meal and our children at the same time. After the twins turned two they started joining us for meals.

Morning worship

My husband and I have found that the time together around the breakfast table is the best time to have morning worship. We keep it short—about five to seven minutes—and the whole worship is directed toward the children. As the spiritual leader of our home, my husband always oversees this time. We try to have activities or readings that will encourage the children to think for themselves and to interact during worship.

The children look forward to family worship every morning. They know that breakfast doesn't start until we have it. Our worships always end with one of the children praying, asking the Lord to help us practice what we have learned and thanking the Lord for the food.

Several years ago, we added an intercessory prayer to our routine before family members part for the day. Right before my husband leaves for work, he gathers the family around him and prays for every member. He asks God for our protection. This prayer is always offered by my husband and not by anybody else. He serves as high priest, and just as the Israelite high priest would offer the morning sacrifice, my husband now fulfills a similar task for our family.

Some of you may be single parents, and some may have husbands who do not offer spiritual support. If so, then you can gather your children around you and offer this prayer before you part for the day. Also, if your husband doesn't support family worship, I recommend gathering the children to have a small worship right after the beds are made.

Washing the dishes

It is now eight o'clock, and the family has finished breakfast. It's time to wash the dishes.

A dishwasher makes the job simple. I use a dishwasher the

way most people use the kitchen sink. After a *quick* rinse, the dishes immediately go into the dishwasher. If your children are old enough, each can promptly rinse his own dish and put it in the dishwasher. My children are too young to do this, so I do it myself. Your husband should be able to help too.

I can't understand why so many women wash the dishes by hand before putting them in a dishwasher. Why have a dishwasher? Why the wasted effort? When we first moved to a house with a dishwasher, I never used it. Everyone I knew washed the dishes by hand before putting them in the dishwasher, and that didn't make sense to me. Finally, I decided to use it, but only if it worked my way. I threw out the big chunks of food, did a fast rinse, and put the dishes in the dishwasher. It worked! The dishes were just as clean as if I had washed them by hand!

Perhaps some think of a dishwasher as a sterilizing instrument. A dishwasher does not effectively kill bacteria; it simply washes dishes automatically instead of your washing them by hand.

I realize that some dishwashers do a better job than others, and this will affect how much rinsing needs to be done before loading the machine. Still I don't believe I have to wash dishes twice. Learn how to make your appliances work for your benefit and give you more time.

For those who don't have a dishwasher, fill up the sink with hot, sudsy water before the meal. As soon as family members are through eating, they can rinse their dishes and put them in the hot, soapy water. Then go dress the children or do something else for a while. When it's time to return to the dishes, they will be easy to clean quickly.

A few more things to do

I clean the kitchen and dress the children between eight and nine o'clock. That's all I am able to do in one hour. For those who have children who must be driven to school or to the bus stop, please read the chapter for working women. There, I explain how to prepare for the early-morning drive. Much of what follows here will apply to women who are at home and who have small children.

I don't recommend trying to accomplish more than two tasks in one hour. One woman called me, totally frustrated that she was never able to accomplish her homemaking goals. She described six jobs she planned to do in two hours that morning and asked if I thought that was too much. I had to tell her she would not be able to do it all. I suggested three jobs to do in those two hours.

If the tasks are simple and not time consuming, you may be able to do more than two jobs in one hour, but if they are more involved, you may be able to do only one job per hour. On the average, aim at two short tasks in one hour. Dealing with children and their problems takes much attention during that hour. Cramming too much into a short time only leads to frustration and unnecessary time pressure

And now I can do what I want!

At nine o'clock I stop to look around. The whole house is tidy, my children and I are dressed and ready for the day's activities, *and it is only nine in the morning*!

I now have from nine o'clock to eleven-thirty to do anything I want or need to do. I can take the children to the park or on a walk. I can go shopping. I can visit a friend. I can fold laundry. I don't have to clean anything in the house. Hard to believe, isn't it?

Many Christian mothers have a great burden for their children's spiritual well-being. They wonder, "How can I spend meaningful time with my children when I have so much to clean in the house?" If you follow a Sabbath-preparation plan like the one I outline, you will be able to spend time with your children when they are the most active and alert.

Lunch and supper

At eleven-thirty, I prepare for lunch. It doesn't matter how simple the meal is, it is still a chore if you aren't prepared and organized. Here is how I prepare for lunch and supper.

It's always easier to prepare meals when we know what we are going to do ahead of time. Preparing meals becomes difficult when we walk into the kitchen near mealtime, wondering what we will cook.

Imagine, with me, a typical housewife who prepares her meals at the last minute. As she pulls out her pots and pans, she starts to have ideas of what she will make for supper. Just as she gets started, she realizes that she is missing some of the ingredients needed for her entree. So she thinks of another dish to prepare, but then realizes she is missing ingredients for that dish too. Sooner or later she turns up with something to eat, possibly after having to go to the store to buy necessary ingredients. She is now upset as she quickly throws everything together, muttering all the while about what a pain it is to feed the family.

Preparing meals for your family is a serious thing that requires serious thought. The physical health and welfare of your family depends to a great degree on the food they eat. Children's bodies are growing and developing. Husbands work hard and need good nutrition to keep up their health and strength. Cooking is a very important aspect of your job as a homemaker.

How can cooking be made easier? By knowing ahead of time what to make for the meal. Some cooks can keep all their meal plans in their mind. They know what they will cook on specific days, with no need of a written reminder. Most of us are not that way. We need to have a written reminder of what we will make and when we will make it. A written menu doesn't always save money, but I believe it does save time.

I approach this menu by thinking of what my family enjoys eating, and I try to please each member by fixing favorite dishes sometime during the week. I consider the schedules and time constraints of my husband and the other family members. If there is time, I try to be more creative. If I am pressured for time, then one-dish meals or quick fixer-uppers will take precedence. I may leave something to cook in the crock-pot through the night. Whatever the meal, I make sure it is nutritious.

Here is what I mean by one-dish meals. They are meals that can be cooked in one pan or pot. These dishes don't need anything on the side, so I don't fix anything else to go with them. All nutrients and food groups can be found in a one-dish meal. Examples of one-dish meals include stir-fry vegetables over brown rice, burritos, or haystacks.

My menus are not like restaurant or school cafeteria menus. Next to each dish, I write the ingredients that I will need. For example:

Busy Woman's Lasagna:
    1 cup cottage cheese   1 jar Ragu spaghetti sauce
    1 cup Parmesan cheese   1 bag of pasta
    1 can sliced olives

Vegetables:
    Broccoli and cauliflower

Salad:
    Lettuce   Tomatoes
    Carrots   Artichokes
    Blue cheese dressing

Bread:
    Garlic bread

Drink:
    Apple juice with 7UP

I write out the menu with a list of ingredients the night before I go shopping so I won't forget anything. The list of ingredients really helps me when I make the shopping list. All this may take a little more time initially, but I won't be running back to the store in the middle of the week to buy something I forgot! I know some women who go to the store daily, and others have to go three or four times a week to get something for one of their meals. You can avoid all this with careful planning.

Once the menu is written, stick to it as much as possible. Always think ahead. Look at the menu the night before to see if you can do anything to help gain time for the next day. Get those beans out and let them soak all night so it will be easy to start cooking them the next morning. I usually start working on supper in the morning so that I won't feel rushed.

As I plan my menu, I also consider what food I need in case I am not able to make the meal I planned. Canned soups, dried noodle soups, and canned fruit are useful foods to have in the pantry when plans go awry. I have often used these foods with bread to make a quick and nutritious meal when my menu plans have failed.

Monday a light day

Now that lunch is done, what else do I have to do to make Friday the lightest day of the week? Not very much! Monday is usually a light day for me, and I want it to be a light day for you too. I try to do something fun with the children after they get up from their naps. Sometimes I take a nap myself.

It is important, however, to tidy up the house in the evening. With a tidy house, you will be happy to get up the next morning. You are on your way to being prepared for a new Sabbath!

Chapter 5

Feeling Free by Friday

So far, you may be having difficulty understanding how all we've been discussing fits together into a plan for Sabbath preparation. Don't worry; it will all fall into place soon. Let's continue now through the rest of the work week.

Tuesday—shopping day

It's now Tuesday morning. On Tuesday, I take care of beds and breakfast and dishes just as I do on Monday—except for one thing. Before I put the dishes in the dishwasher, I thoroughly clean out the refrigerator. Why? Because today I go grocery shopping! I shop every Tuesday, preferably in the morning.

Many women are surprised at this. "Why shop so early in the week?" they ask. Many shop on Friday and still try to have all their cooking completed before Sabbath. A few who think ahead go shopping on Thursday. For me, Thursday or Friday is too late to shop for groceries and still be truly relaxed and prepared for the Sabbath hours.

In an article on Sabbath keeping ("How to Keep the Sabbath," *Spectrum*, August 1988, p. 50), Charles Scriven wrote: "Never lose sight . . . of the reasons for Sabbathkeeping; never lose sight of what it is you are trying to preserve." He follows with this illustration:

We [my wife Marianne and I] happened to be talking

55

about the Sabbath while rushing through some last-minute cooking—after Friday sundown. Feeling suddenly repentant, Marianne said, "It's not that God will punish us for this, it's that we cheat ourselves."

Her remark illuminates our attitude to Sabbath keeping. A gift has come to us, the gift of the Sabbath. God is not waiting around to zap us at the first sign of our misusing the gift, but if we do misuse it, we dishonor the Giver—by cheating ourselves out of the songs and prayers together, out of the restful celebration, out of the opportunity for deeds of kindness.

But if, on the other hand, we treat the Sabbath well, if we honor it, if we stop and remember in the doing, then we will find wholeness. The Sabbath will cease being merely a collection of rules and become what God intended the Sabbath to be, a jubilee of the world.

Preparation for shopping

While cleaning out the refrigerator, I open every container. I throw away unnecessary items and place the empty dishes in the sink. After years of doing this, I have finally figured out the primary purpose of a refrigerator. We use it to store all those leftovers that we feel guilty about throwing away! Last week, the broccoli looked too good to dump. Now it looks pretty bad, so it's much easier to throw out. Now it doesn't hurt my conscience!

I clean all the racks and the walls of the refrigerator. I straighten out the freezer so that everything looks neat and clean. Now I put back all the items that go in the refrigerator. Besides the breakfast dishes, I've filled the sink with dishes from the refrigerator, so now I clean them all at the same time.

At nine o'clock I'm off to the market with my shopping list, my purse, and my children. I use the menu (I wrote it out the night before, remember?) to prepare my grocery list.

Most of us follow a particular path through the supermarket aisles. So why not arrange your list in the same order that you will encounter the aisles with those items? For example, I come to the produce section first, so the first items on my list are produce items. As a further way to make sure I don't forget certain food sections in the market while I'm writing my list, I put the actual aisle names on my list in the order that I come to them (PRODUCE, DAIRY PRODUCTS, BAKERY, etc.). This serves as a good memory jogger. Try it, and see how it will help organize your shopping. One other thing: I make sure that my route through the market ends in the frozen-food section because that way frozen items will have less time to melt. It's not fun to come home with dripping packages!

Refrigerator and pantry organization

I'm always looking for ways to save time or to make things easier, so I try many different ideas. One shopping idea that has been working for me lately is to put away the groceries at the same time that I bring them into the house. I take two grocery bags out of the car, bring them into the house, and put those groceries away. Then I return to the car to get two more bags, and I continue doing this until all the groceries are put away. The result? I don't end up with wall-to-wall grocery bags in my kitchen, cluttering up the counters, blocking cabinets, and generally making it more difficult to put away the groceries. Now I notice, too, how much it helps to have cleaned the refrigerator prior to shopping. I can put away the things that need to go into the refrigerator without further crowding or hassle.

I have certain places for every item in my refrigerator—for the fruit, the vegetables, etc. I have several reasons for this. First, it helps me use refrigerator space more efficiently, and I have more room for storage. Second, it makes it easier for the children to help me put groceries away. Third, it allows me to see quickly when I am low on a certain item, thereby helping me when I write the shopping list. Fourth, it prevents spoilage of certain food items that would be hidden behind a disorganized group of containers.

I also carefully organize the pantry. I divide it into sections, and each item has its place. My reasons for organizing the pantry are the same as for the refrigerator. Keep in mind that all this organization makes it possible to have a more rested Sabbath.

Cleaning out the refrigerator and shopping are the only jobs that make Tuesday morning different from the other days of the week. Isn't it nice to have shopping out of the way so early in the week!

I use the rest of Tuesday as I please. Sometimes I have errands to run. Sometimes I may visit a friend or take the children for a walk.

Most important, don't forget to tidy up in the evening. It will make tomorrow a much easier day.

Wednesday—a day to enjoy

Now it's Wednesday, and do you know what big job I have planned for today? *Nothing!* After I finish the early-morning ritual and the dishes are washed, I'm on my own!

No woman should feel like a slave in her own home. So many women complain about not having any time for themselves. They feel that they work for the family without reward or relief. No one seems to care about what happens to them. Resentment and frustration build over the years. To prevent this burnout, it's important to make time for yourself, even to pamper yourself a bit. Many women tell me that the idea of a free day in the middle of the week really appeals to them. Shouldn't you relax and enjoy life?

If you run out of ideas for what to do on the day off, how about the following?

1. Write a letter.
2. Enjoy a hobby or craft.
3. Play with the kids or take them on a field trip.
4. Leave the kids with a baby sitter and go away for the day.
5. Go window shopping.
6. Invite friends over to the house.

Don't forget to tidy up in the evening. Tomorrow, Thursday, will be a very important day.

Thursday—Sabbath cleanup

Now that I am rested from having Wednesday off, I can tackle Thursday. Today is the day to really think about Sabbath preparation. More than on any other day, my children notice the nearness of the Sabbath as they see me perform Thursday's activities. Over the years, my children have learned to anticipate the Sabbath with joy.

Since most women use Friday for their major Sabbath preparation, often rushing around trying the beat the clock, Friday has unfortunately become a very negative day for many children. We are in such a hurry to get our work done on Friday that we spend no time with the kids. If you start your preparation on Thursday, however, you won't feel as much time pressure, and you will be able to spend more quality time with your children.

After breakfast, I do more than just tidy up the kitchen. I clean it thoroughly. I put the breakfast dishes in the dishwasher or wash them by hand. Then I fill the sink with hot water and put degreaser into the water. I also put degreaser all around the stove. Then I take the stove elements that lie over the burners and put them in the hot water to soak.

Next I grab the spray cleanser (Fantastik, Formula 409, e.g.), and I spray all my appliances. I spray the microwave oven, scrub it down, and then rinse it. I spray, scrub, and rinse the toaster after dumping all the crumbs. I spray, scrub, and rinse all the counters and the kitchen table. Next, I place the kitchen towels with the load of laundry to be washed. I spray, scrub, and rinse the outside of the refrigerator, remembering to clean the top. People over six feet tall, like my husband, don't enjoy looking at a grimy refrigerator top. I don't have to worry about the inside of the refrigerator. Remember, I cleaned it on Tuesday. Isn't that nice?

When the rest of the kitchen is clean, I scrub the stove. This doesn't take too much effort because degreaser has been on the surface all this time. Then I move to the sink and start cleaning the stove elements. I scrub them really well, dry them off, and put them back on the stove. I clear off all the counters and replace the kitchen towels with clean ones.

I stand back and admire the kitchen. Doesn't it look lovely? I sweep the kitchen floor, but I don't mop it yet. It is now about nine or nine-thirty in the morning. Sure, it took longer to do the kitchen cleaning, but now the kitchen is ready for Sabbath. The children haven't bothered me much since they were happily playing this morning. They are usually ready to play for a long time after breakfast. I sing Christian songs as I'm cleaning, maintaining a light and happy attitude. Sometimes the children come to talk to me while I'm cleaning, and I answer their questions. I tell them that we're preparing our house for the Lord so that we can be ready for His special day. They get excited.

Believe it or not, I don't do anything else extra this morning after I completely clean the kitchen.

Thursday afternoon—cleaning the bathrooms

After lunch, while the kids are napping or resting, I take advantage of their inactivity by cleaning the bathrooms. Whether you have one or ten bathrooms in your house, you should clean them all at this time. Cleaning bathrooms is much more difficult when I have to keep one eye on the children. It takes time to make sure they aren't drinking the Lysol. It's easy to become impatient when they put their muddy shoes in the recently cleaned tub or when they walk in the shower with the Ajax in the stall. At this point it's easy to get upset, start perspiring, and scream at the kids. I spare myself all that anxiety by tackling the bathrooms when the children are resting in their bedrooms.

I keep cleaning utensils and materials—Lysol, Ajax, Windex, paper towels, scrub brushes, etc.—in each bathroom. That way I don't have to lug things from room to room, possibly forgetting to bring some items with me. It's a pain to run back to a bathroom I have just cleaned to get something I need. If it isn't possible for you to have all your cleaning materials in every bathroom, then I suggest keeping the items in a partitioned carrying case and carrying it from bathroom to bathroom.

Before doing anything else, I go to each individual bathroom and pour some bleach into the commodes and let it sit there. Then I begin cleaning each bathroom. I start by washing the sink. I always scrub the sink with some type of cleanser; then I rinse. I spray Lysol all over the counter and sink; then I scrub them with a soft towel. This does wonders for my sinks. After finishing with the sink, I go through all the drawers in the counter and straighten the contents.

I know a simple way to organize the bathroom drawers. I use flatware dividers—the same ones you use in your kitchen drawers for your flatware. These dividers come in different sizes, so there is one that will fit just about any size of bathroom drawer. I have one divider in my bathroom drawer, and my husband has another one in his. The toothpaste goes in the "knife" section, the combs go in the "fork" section, and so on. If you will do this, the drawers will require little straightening because the items don't slide around in the drawer.

After finishing the sink, I start on the tub. I clean it the same way I cleaned the sink. First I scrub the whole tub with some type of cleanser; then I rinse. I spray Lysol on the tub and scrub it down with a towel. I clean all the tub fixtures too. If the tub has a shower curtain, I recommend spraying a disinfectant like Lysol on the bottom of the curtain—the part that comes in contact with the tub. This prevents mildew.

Now, to the commode. Remember that I put bleach in each commode at the beginning? This now makes it easy to brush the bowl. I then spray the outside of the commode with my trusty Lysol, and I scrub all the surfaces.

I take all the towels down so I can wash them. I empty the trash cans and shake out all the rugs. My bathrooms have always been small enough to clean on my hands and knees, so I take a paper towel and pick up all the dust on the floor. I spray a cloth with Lysol and go over the whole floor with it.

Before I leave the bathroom, I clean the mirrors with Windex. Now the bathroom is spotless. I repeat this process in every bathroom, whether big or small.

One time, when my oldest child was three years old, he told me after he awoke from his nap, "Mommy, it smells like Sabbath." His comment surprised me and made me happy. He had figured out after three short years of life that Sabbath is a special time worth preparing for. You can cement these positive experiences in your children's minds.

I finish with the bathrooms at around two or two-thirty in the afternoon. The children finish their naps at about the same time. Now, believe it or not, I have the rest of the afternoon for myself and the kids. I don't do major cleaning when the kids are awake.

Thursday night—the cleaning is finished

After I have tidied up the house and put the children to bed, I have two main jobs yet to do to complete the Sabbath cleaning.

First, I mop the kitchen floor. The kids are in bed, so I'm able to do it much faster than if they were up. Also, there is no one around to walk on the wet floor and slip on it. Next I polish the furniture. For an hour, I go from room to room and dust every article of furniture. If the furniture has glass, I use Windex. When I dust and polish the furniture in the children's rooms, I also straighten out their toys and put their sets of books in the proper order.

The house is now ready for the Sabbath—and it is only Thursday night! Unbelievable, isn't it?

Many Adventist women are thrilled when they start putting this plan into practice. A few weeks after I had given my seminar at a particular church, a young woman came running to me as I walked in the door. She threw her arms around me and said, "I did it! I did it! I never thought I could, but I did it! I've never had a more restful Sabbath, and my house has never been so clean as it was this week! Thank you so much! Thank you so much!"

Notice what I have *not* done as I have gotten the house all ready for Sabbath by Thursday night. I have not taken time from the children. They were never in my way. I was free to be with them in the morning and afternoon.

I must admit that I have this system down so pat that if I juggle a little with the schedule, I can be done with all the cleaning before supper on Thursday night. At first it may take you a long time to do everything, but after a while you can do the job in half the time.

What about the wash?

No, I didn't forget about the wash, even though sometimes I wish I could. It would be nice to say that doing the wash is no big deal and that it is no problem to keep up with. The wash takes time, but it doesn't have to be an overwhelming experience. It all depends on how it is done.

There are three main ways of doing the wash. The worst way is to wash the clothes, put them in the dryer, remove them from the dryer, and then throw them on the bed or sofa. It's a horrible feeling to realize that something must be done about that mountain of wrinkled clothing.

The second way is not the worst, but neither is it the best. Instead of throwing the clothing on the bed after washing and drying, you can carefully lay each article flat on the bed in a way that prevents wrinkling. But you will still have to fold the clothes and put them away eventually. This takes a long time.

The best way is the way most women resist because they think it takes more time. Believe me, it doesn't. The best way is to wash, then dry, then fold, and then put away the clothes all in one operation. Try it, and you'll find it's easier and less time-consuming than doing it piecemeal.

I do one or two loads of wash a day. One load contains all the colorful clothing. The next load contains all the dark clothing. I wait to accumulate a full load of white clothing so that I can go through the whole bleaching routine with a full load. I don't fold the white clothes; I roll them. This seems like the military to many people, but it looks so much neater and it allows much more room in the drawer.

If you follow the best way of doing the wash, you will never have messy drawers. As I put the clothing away, I straighten out the drawer. Since I do the wash daily, the drawers always remain neat. I usually put one load in after breakfast; the second load goes in after the first one is done. Of course, I fold the clothes and put them away quickly. I also have hangers in the washroom to hang up clothing as soon as it comes out of the dryer. I seldom iron anything. Each night before bedtime, I put a load of wash into the washing machine, or, at least, I sort the clothes to be washed the next day. The schedule should allow plenty of time in the morning, afternoon, or night to wash clothes. My ideas for the working woman, presented in chapter 7, include ways to plan for washing clothes. These ideas may also help the busy woman who stays at home.

I reserve Thursdays for towel and rug washing. I wash throw rugs about once or twice every three months. It's nice to have clean, sweet-smelling towels for the Sabbath

Don't try to catch up

Let me give you one more piece of advice that will make a big difference as you prepare for the Sabbath. If you weren't able to accomplish a major cleaning task on a particular day for one reason or another, don't worry. Don't try to catch up. All this will do is put you behind and make you frustrated.

For example, if I'm not able to clean the stove on Thursday, I won't try to do it on Friday. That will only mess up Friday because I have added a task that I hadn't planned for. Instead, I will wait for next Thursday and do it then.

This applies to all cleaning, but it doesn't apply to grocery shopping. Obviously, you can't put off eating for one week (although it would be nice to be taken out to dinner during that time!).

Friday—changing the sheets

On Friday, I follow the same early-morning routine; however, there is one exception. Before making the beds, I change the sheets on each one. My children know that the changing of the sheets is another clue to the soon arrival of the Sabbath. I wash the dirty sheets that morning or sometime during the weekend. I also put out clean bath towels that morning.

The house is now at the peak of cleanliness for the Sabbath. Now we can concentrate on preparing our children for a positive Sabbath experience.

Chapter 6

The Real Sabbath Preparation

Now it's time to start working on the "real" Sabbath preparation. Just because your house is all clean by Friday—may, in fact, have never been cleaner—doesn't mean that you are through preparing for the Sabbath. The physical side of Sabbath preparation is very important, but the real Sabbath preparation is a spiritual preparation. This is what will make the Sabbath the highlight of the week for your family. You want to enjoy the Sabbath to its fullest extent—and that involves preparing your heart as well as your home. Maybe you've been so busy trying to get your home ready for Sabbath that you haven't had time to think about getting your heart ready. Real Sabbath preparation involves preparing your heart to receive the blessing God intends for you on that day.

To prepare ourselves for the Sabbath, we need to deal with these issues that can disturb our Sabbath joy: (1) disagreements with others; (2) lack of Bible study; (3) lack of prayer throughout the week; (4) preoccupation with secular activities; (5) exhaustion; and (6) overinvolvement in church activities. These may sound like trite clichés. You may wonder if these things really have much of an effect. Take my word for it, they have a tremendous impact.

Disagreements with others

Have you ever gone to a wedding or a party after having had

65

a big argument with your spouse? It's hard to enjoy the festivities with all the negative thoughts going through your mind, isn't it? "I don't know what's wrong with my husband. How could he have accused me the way he did?" Or "I'm so tired of the house being such a mess, and it's all because my husband isn't doing his part." You probably felt like going home. Those same emotions can block the happiness that we should have on Sabbath.

Sometimes it almost seems that the enemy plans emotional turmoil with our spouses just a couple of days before the Sabbath so that we will miss out on its blessings. Satan knows us so well. He knows our weaknesses, and he exploits them time after time. If we are quick-tempered, we can almost be sure of a fight every Sabbath morning with our spouse. We can see Satan at work, trying to ruin our Sabbath.

So, if we are to go to church with a clear mind and a glad heart, we must make things right with our spouse. This is easier said than done. Making things right calls for a spirit of humility, understanding, and love at every level of communication. Sharing the things that truly hurt us and making ourselves vulnerable are not easy. Saying, "I'm sorry. I was wrong. Please forgive me," comes hard, but only through a spirit of humility can we receive what the Lord has in store for us. God will help us make things right.

It may be even harder to settle disagreements with a child than with a spouse—particularly an older child or teenager. But children, young or old, will have more respect for the parent who is strong enough to say, "I made a mistake. I misjudged you. I'm sorry," than for the parent who is too proud to admit he or she was wrong. Again, it's a matter of humility, understanding, and love. Our children can learn how to prepare spiritually for the Sabbath only from us.

Lack of Bible study

"I am not being fed at church!" "My pastor's sermons are terrible!" "He has nothing to say to the congregation!" You've heard these statements before, and perhaps you've made them yourself. They indicate a serious problem.

Not every pastor is a gifted orator. Preaching may be a weak area for some, although they have strengths in other aspects of ministry. Does this mean that you should leave the church because you're not being fed? Do you feel that someone has to spoon-feed you every week, lest you die of spiritual malnutrition?

You cannot depend wholly on your pastor for spiritual growth. Christians have to take responsibility for their own spiritual nourishment as well as drawing on the reserves of others. You will receive benefit from church only in proportion to what you have gained spiritually during the week. If you neglect to study the Bible for yourself, if you fail to let the Holy Spirit touch your life through a personal encounter with God's Word, then you will remain a spiritual baby. The Sabbath and the worship service will have little meaning for you. Your pastor may be an excellent preacher or a mediocre one. In either case, it is your own individual Bible study throughout the week that will result in lasting benefit for your spiritual growth.

Lack of prayer throughout the week

Only the Holy Spirit can bring spiritual change to the life. And the Holy Spirit brings that change in answer to prayer. The more you pray, the more everything around you will be different. You will see things with a different perspective, with a more understanding heart. Your Sabbath experience will be enhanced through prayer during the week.

Pray for your pastor. The more time you spend praying for him, the less time you will spend being critical of him. During the week, pray for the blessing that you hope to receive on Sabbath. God will not disappoint you.

Preoccupation with secular activities

We all need to take care of our secular responsibilities. Unfortunately, they can easily crowd into our lives, take over, and disturb our spiritual Sabbath preparation. In His parable of the sower and the seed, Jesus said that thorns choked some of the plants that sprang up from the good seed. These thorns, He said, represent the "cares of the world." These secular activities can disturb our Sabbath communion with Him.

If you become too busy and preoccupied with these "cares of the world," two things will happen. You will become so tired that you will look forward to Sabbath for the physical rest alone. You will also have your mind cluttered with so many activities and problems that you will be distracted during the Sabbath School and the worship service.

Overinvolvement with church activities

Can we ever do too much for the Lord? It seems that the answer should be No, but just as we can be preoccupied with secular activities, we can also be overly involved with the sacred. This, too, takes its toll. Consider, for instance, the active church member who carries many responsibilities. During the worship service, her mind may wander as she thinks of the vespers program she is planning, the Pathfinder fair the next day, the Home and School meeting coming up. Perhaps those four Bible studies she gives every week hardly leave her time for her husband and family.

Is it possible to be so busy working for the Lord that we fail to hear His voice? I believe it is. At one point, I did so much for the church that all day Sabbath I would run around, fulfilling responsibilities at my own church and at others in the area. I became very unhappy in the midst of all my "good deeds."

Here is another pitfall that I learned about from personal experience. Since my Fridays became so light under my schedule, I filled the time with a lot of miscellaneous activities—some secular and others for the church. Eventually, I put so many things off for Friday that Fridays became very hectic. I wasn't cleaning my house on Friday, but I was running around all day doing other things. Consequently, I was no better off for using my Sabbath-preparation system. I had neglected my spiritual Sabbath preparation. If you find yourself with light Fridays, don't fill them with activities that will take away from your spiritual Sabbath preparation.

Please don't misunderstand. It's our privilege to work for God, and we should let Him use us. But if overinvolvement is turning your Sabbath into a business, then you are missing out. Too much of the Lord's work on the Lord's day will spoil the joy.

Exhaustion

Sabbath provides both physical and spiritual relief from our weekly endeavors. If you don't plan your week right and leave all Sabbath preparation for Friday, you will be very tired when Sabbath arrives. How can you hear the sermon when you're nodding off to sleep? The Lord wants your mind to be clear so that you can see His works clearly and find His love for you through His creation. How can you do this if you are running around on Friday, trying to put a whole week's worth of work into one day? Friday becomes a day of chaos as you frantically try to beat the clock toward sundown, or you may simply give up and say, "So what?" as Sabbath comes while you are trying to get ready. But if you use at least some of the ideas in this book, you should be able to have some time for the preparation of your mind and heart throughout the week and on Friday. The Sabbath can be a delight!

Sabbath preparation and young children

If you have children at home, you need to prepare their minds for the Sabbath. This will take effort and planning, since children are so wrapped up with their play. If nothing else, physically preparing the house for Sabbath helps them get into a frame of mind for what is to come.

How we teach our children about the Sabbath is very important, and we need to be careful how we go about it. My goal right now is to make Sabbath so special for my children that they would never think of living without it. During Friday, I ask the children many questions.

"Why do I take the time to make everything special for the Sabbath?"

"Why is it an important day?"

"Why did God make the Sabbath?"

"Why do we go to church on the Sabbath?"

"What will we do at church tomorrow?"

I let them freely answer these questions. I try to make sure that the expression on my face portrays the joy that comes from making a special time for the Lord. I explain how our family will try to keep our activities centered around Jesus because we want it to be His day. I sing some of the Sabbath School songs so that their little hearts will be filled with anticipation and joy. I give them time to explain their Sabbath

School lesson to me, and we go over their memory verse. All these things help prepare them spiritually for the Sabbath.

We open the Sabbath hours with worship, trying to accomplish what Ellen White recommends in *Child Guidance*: "Before the setting of the sun, let the members of the family assemble to read God's word, to sing and pray. . . . We should begin anew to make special arrangements that every member of the family may be prepared to honor the day which God has blessed and sanctified" (p. 529).

The Sabbath and teenagers

Many teenagers complain that older people never explain the reasons why they do the things they do. Young people easily become frustrated with practices that make no sense to them, and this frustration may lead to rebellion. I believe that if we explain our values to our children when they are young, they will be less likely to rebel against them when they are teenagers. The teen years are naturally a time when our children question and rebel in many areas of life and religious faith. This process is, in some ways, a normal part of growing up. We should be ready with reasonable answers to their questions.

What if your teenagers are not willing to cooperate with your new Sabbath-preparation plan? What can you do? Here are some ideas.

First, fervently pray about this matter. Ask the Lord to give you ideas on how to get support from your family.

Then share with your teenagers how you are convicted that the Lord's day should be made more meaningful for the family. Share some of your ideas and let them share some of theirs. Often they will think of many fine ideas. Let them talk about their frustrations with Sabbath keeping. What is it that they don't understand? What inconsistencies do they perceive? What makes it hard for them to keep the Sabbath? Ask the Lord to guide you in what to say. Perhaps your teenagers will learn to see the Sabbath in a new light.

Once, a teenager asked me why he couldn't do what he wanted to do on the Sabbath. It was a free day for him, so why couldn't he do as he wished? I told him that the day was intended for us to get to know God and give Him glory. Then I asked him, "How would you feel if all your friends wished you a happy birthday in the morning and then did nothing the rest of the day to make you feel that it was your special day? What if you got no gifts, had no party to which you could invite your friends, or didn't even have your favorite meal served for dinner? Let's say you asked your mom if she had anything planned for that day, and she told you she was looking forward to spending it doing fun things with *her* friends! How would you feel? Whose special day would it be then?" His body language told me that he understood what I meant.

The purpose of Sabbath preparation

Sabbath preparation involves much more than getting the house in shape before sunset on Friday evening. After all, you can have the cleanest and most organized house in town, but if your heart and those of your family are not right with God and with one another, there is no blessing to be gained from the clean house.

Preparing your mind and heart is made easier by an ongoing, daily devotional experience that culminates with the Sabbath. Your appreciation for the Sabbath and for the Lord will grow as you prepare your houses and your heart for Him.

Chapter 7

Help for the Working Woman

Several years ago I gave my seminar on Sabbath preparation to a group of working women. It was a great eye-opener for me. I got a glimpse of the magnitude of responsibility that falls on the working woman. (In this chapter, I will use the term *working woman* as a kind of shorthand for the woman who is employed outside the home. Please understand that I don't at all mean to imply that full-time homemakers are not also "working women.")

"What can I share with this special group of women that will be beneficial?" I asked myself when the invitation came. I thought of telling everyone to hire a maid! But of course that isn't a practical solution for most working women. After much prayer, I tried to put myself in a working woman's shoes. I also interviewed many working women. As a result, I have to say to all you women who are employed outside the home, "My hat is off to you." You have a very difficult task, especially if you are also a mother.

In the seminar, I asked the working women to try my ideas to see if they would work for them. I received very positive feedback. I am sure the ideas in this book—and especially in this chapter—can help many working women, regardless of their situation. In saying that, I don't minimize the difficulties. No matter how attractively I present it, my plan obviously requires effort to carry out. Whether a woman *will* carry it out depends on her priorities and how much she wants to enhance the Sabbath experience for herself and her family.

Sabbath preparation and the working woman

I realize it's easy for the working woman to say, "I'm doing the best I can. The Lord understands what I go through every week." Yes, the Lord understands how difficult everything has become in this hectic life. But do we understand the importance of the Sabbath experience—for us and, particularly, for our children? Are we content to deny ourselves the positive experience we can have from the Sabbath?

Some working women reading this chapter may now be experiencing the "empty-nest syndrome." You suffer from loneliness now that your children have grown and left the home. You may be tempted to say, "I don't need to make anything special out of the Sabbath anymore. I only need to think about my husband and me."

When you work all week and do little or nothing about preparing for the Sabbath, then it becomes just like any other day. Sure, you can go to church on the Sabbath, but if that is all that distinguishes the Sabbath from the rest of the week, then some of the joy of the Sabbath died for you when your children left. The Sabbath is not just a holiday for children. It's a holy day—a special day—for all of us, even working women.

What if you are a working mother? Even though it will take time and discipline, you can still maintain the home and make it special for the Sabbath hours.

Then there is the working single parent. This woman is now alone as she struggles to meet her obligations. If this is your situation, you need the Sabbath more than ever. It may be the only hours you have to solidify the social and spiritual ties with your family, your church, and your God. If you make it a special day, it can be a time that lifts up your family spiritually.

Whatever category of working woman you fit into, the following ideas will be beneficial as you deal with the important task of Sabbath preparation.

Husbands

I haven't mentioned husbands so far in this chapter. I have

a reason for that. Many working women are fortunate to have husbands who help them with the burden of maintaining a home. Others, however, have husbands who refuse to do "women's work," even though their wives have a full-time job outside the home.

I have written this chapter with this second group of women in mind. Even though you can fairly easily train children to do housework, many husbands are not as adaptable. If your husband is in this category, the ideas in this chapter will make it possible for you to cope with the upkeep of the home.

For those with heavy household burdens and uninterested husbands, I have only one recommendation: pray fervently for the Lord's help. Nagging a reluctant husband is about as useful as hitting your head against a brick wall. You may get some short-term benefits from nagging, but the risk of marital strife is great. Pray not only for your husband but for yourself. Ask the Lord to help you bear your burdens cheerfully and to give you strength sufficient for the job. "They that wait upon the Lord shall renew their strength; they shall mount up with wings as eagles; they shall run, and not be weary; and they shall walk, and not faint" (Isaiah 40:31).

The Holy Spirit can do much to soften the heart of a husband, to help him realize how much you need his help and support. Have the faith to anticipate good results. You may find after a time that you married a good helper after all! Husbands who are willing to help can be easily incorporated into the Sabbath-preparation routine, as their schedules allow.

When should the working woman have her house at the peak of cleanliness? The home may not be at the peak of cleanliness on Friday morning, but it can be orderly and clean by that time. A working woman cannot set Friday as her goal for Sabbath preparation. The working woman's goal should be to have her home clean and tidy throughout the week. Here's how.

The working woman's "night before"

Like the full-time homemaker, the working woman also needs to start with the night before. Your daily goal should be to leave your home thoroughly tidy by bedtime. When I say tidy, I mean there should be no clothes, toys, papers, shoes, or anything else lying around. The rooms where the children are sleeping should be tidy—nothing on the floor, nothing scattered about. One of the most satisfying things I can think of is to go to bed in a tidy house.

Before you go to bed, take a trip to the closet. Pull out what you are going to wear to work the next morning. This is an important step. Choosing your clothes in the morning takes precious time. You may think you know what you'll wear the next day, but when morning comes, it's sometimes another story. All of a sudden, you realize that the blouse you were going to wear is in the wash. Now you have to quickly think up another outfit. This takes time! Maybe you have to quickly do some ironing you hadn't planned on—and your morning is off to a bad start already!

So pull out your clothes so that they're ready to wear tomorrow morning. Do the same with the children's clothes before they go to bed. Then when they get up in the morning to go to school, they will know exactly what to wear and won't need your help at the last minute.

Set the breakfast table the night before to save time in the morning. Prepare the orange juice. The more you do the night before, the more time you will have in the morning.

The working woman needs to use all the devices of our modern age to best advantage. For example, buy a second crock-pot (or two if you don't have one already). Leave one on during the night with a hot cereal for breakfast; when you go to work, leave the other on with that night's supper.

Sometimes unforeseen circumstances will make it impossible to tidy up in the evening. Don't get discouraged! Just tidy up the next evening to get back on the program once more.

The working woman's morning

If any woman needs to make time for devotions, it's the working woman. Somehow you need to find the stamina and the desire to do all that needs to be done at work and at home—and still maintain your relationship with God. It's devotions that help you keep it all together. "Seek ye first the kingdom of God, and his righteousness," Jesus said, "and all these things [the necessities of living] shall be added unto you" (Matthew 6:33).

Get up a few minutes early and tell the Lord all that you need to do. Ask for His help to accomplish the tasks of that day. Do you know what? He will give you the help you ask for!

After devotions and the early-morning routine, put on the clothes that you set out the night before. Make the bed before you walk out of the bedroom. Now the bedroom is ready for the day.

Alarm clocks in each child's room are a help for both the working woman and the full-time homemaker. Children sleep soundly, so put the clock across the room from the bed so they will have to get up to turn it off. Since you have laid out their clothes for them the night before, your children can dress themselves without bothering you. Of course, small children will still need help getting dressed. Older children should come to breakfast all dressed and with their beds made.

After breakfast, every family member clears his section of the table, rinses his dishes, and puts them either in the dishwasher or in hot, sudsy water. If you set the table for supper after breakfast, that will be one less thing to do after coming home from work.

Before the first person leaves the house, gather the family for prayer. If your husband doesn't cooperate, or if you are a single parent, you can pray with the family.

What to do with the kids

When you return from work, you may have children waiting for you at home. If so, they should do some of the household chores before you arrive. This will keep them busy and out of trouble; it will also speed up the evening activities. Here are some things a child can do who is old enough to be home alone after school.

1. Set the supper table if it wasn't done after breakfast.
2. Wash the dishes that were left soaking in hot, sudsy water.
3. Dump the trash.
4. Do their homework.
5. Start fixing supper.
6. Vacuum the house.

Since you left the house tidy in the morning, it should be tidy when you get home. Have an assigned place where the children put their coats, lunch pails, and books when they come home from school. Don't let them throw things on the floor or in the corners.

Too many mothers don't use their children to help at home. Remember that children learn by doing. Also, they will cause less trouble if you keep them busy. I feel strongly that a working mother with teenagers should have little to do at home. When my sister, brothers, and I were in our teens, my father told us that it was our responsibility to give our mother rest. We (girls and boys) did the cooking and cleaning. Some mothers apparently believe the only responsibility their children should have is their schoolwork. I have heard such children as grown-ups voice their resentment because they weren't prepared for the basic skills of life. If you make things too easy for your children, responsibility will be harder on them later on.

As much as possible, try to make the hours at home with the whole family happy moments. During supper, take time to find out what went on during the day with each child. Tell them about your day. Tell them how much you appreciate coming home to be with the family.

After supper, the whole family should help clear the kitchen and set the table for breakfast the next day. The little ones should undress for baths. After their baths, have worship with them, then tuck them into bed with a kiss and a hug. Put out their clothing for tomorrow.

After the older kids finish their homework, they should take their baths and prepare for bed. Encourage them to study their Sabbath School lesson just before they go to bed. Also as a ritual, before they go to bed, ask the children the following questions.

1. Did you bring home from school any papers that I need to see?

2. Do I need to sign any papers?

3. Do I need to write any notes to your teacher?

4. Do I need to send any money with you to school tomorrow?

5. Are you going through any hard times at school that you would like to share with me?

Make sure that each child stacks up his school items and any papers he needs to return in a neat pile. Put lunch money in purses and wallets. That way, everything will be ready in the morning, and there will be no delays. Have the older kids double-check their closets to make sure their clothes for the next day are ready. When they go to bed, their rooms must be neat and tidy.

I believe that children, as far as possible, should aid their mother and be responsible. They can do much on their own. (See the list of appropriate responsibilities for different ages at the end of this chapter.) The evenings will be full for the working woman, but you shouldn't be doing all your work and theirs too.

Evening activities

What should you do in the evenings? It all depends on how relaxed you want to be when Sabbath comes. Here are some ideas for each evening:

Monday evening. Clean the inside of the refrigerator.

Tuesday evening. Go grocery shopping.

Wednesday evening. Clean the kitchen and dust the furniture.

Thursday evening. Clean all bathrooms and mop.

Friday. Change sheets in the morning; vacuum before sunset.

As a working woman, you've worked hard all week. As much as possible, you should have the weekend free of housework to relax and spend the weekend with your family.

The wash

The wash always seems to mess things up. Life would be so much easier if our clothes didn't get dirty! But the clothes must be washed, so let's talk about how the working woman handles this chore.

Wash one load a day, and more if possible. Leave one load washing while you go to bed or when you go to work in the morning. When you return from work, put the load in the dryer, then fold the clothes and put them away. This could be a good chore for teenagers when they come home from school. That same evening, do another load of wash if possible. Dry the load, fold it, and put it away before bedtime. Then you can put another load in the wash before going to bed and repeat the whole process again the next day. This method will help you keep up with the wash throughout the week and, at the same time, avoid the time-consuming task of having to fold a mountain of clothes. The secret of the wash is not when to do it or how much to wash. It is to fold and put away all garments right away!

A friend of mine built five shelflike baskets in her washroom. Each basket belongs to a person in the family. When she folds the clothes, she puts the garments in their respective basket shelves. Each family member is then responsible to pick up his clothes from the basket shelf, carry them to his room, and then put every garment away carefully. This idea may work for you.

Food hints

The working woman deserves time to relax and enjoy her family. As far as possible, every woman, working in or out of the home, should not have to feel that she is in a "no win" situation, a prisoner to the stove. We spend enough time in the kitchen as it is, particularly on weekends. Let me suggest some ways to cut down on kitchen time.

I encourage working women to have set menus for Sunday meals. It's easier on the mind and reduces unnecessary planning to know what to cook ahead of time. Some women have spaghetti every Sunday. You can change the menu every six months or every quarter for variety.

As the working woman looks ahead to a week of cooking, a menu will make her job easier. With a menu, your evenings will be more organized and smooth. A menu will help you know what to prepare the night before for the next morning or what to prepare in the morning for the following supper.

I don't encourage drastically altering the weekly menu. Even though I don't work outside the home, I keep my menus basic, and I don't change them much. I make sure that all the meals are nutritious and that there is enough variety. If the menu doesn't change that much, it will make shopping and cooking much faster and easier on you.

One thing more. Make lunches the night before. This will give you more time in the morning. And your children should prepare their own sack lunches. When I taught second grade, I had a little girl in my class who came from a family of seven children. This seven-year-old prepared her own sack lunch. If a seven-year-old can do it, other children can do it too. I have found that children from big families are more prepared for life's responsibilities because they are made to be responsible early on. Too often, children from smaller families rely solely on good old Mom.

The working woman with no children

The load is much lighter for the single working woman or the woman with no children. For the first four years of our married life, my husband and I had no children. I worked full time as an elementary-school teacher. My home-maintenance plan was different during those years. Still, I never made Sunday a cleaning day. My goal has always been to have the house at the peak of cleanliness for Sabbath. When Monday came around and I had to go to work, I was very relaxed. I had enjoyed the weekend with my husband. It was important for me to have a relaxed weekend before I faced thirty-two second graders on Monday morning!

Of course, cleaning the house was no big deal during those years. I always picked up in the evening. Just because there were only a few things to pick up, I still didn't let them pile up. When we went to bed, the house was tidy.

Sometimes, it's tempting to leave tasks for later when there isn't much work to do. You should resist that temptation, because your neglect will often make the tasks harder to complete later on.

When I didn't have children and worked outside the home, I did all my cleaning on Thursday evenings. As soon as I came home from work, I started a load of wash. I began with the sheets. The second load was all towels. By the time supper was over, I was ready to wash a load of clothing. As I waited for washing cycles to complete and drying times to finish, I would clean the bathroom, dust the furniture, or clean the kitchen. By the time I went to bed on Thursday night, I was ready for the Sabbath. The only thing I needed to do on Friday was vacuum when I got home. I had all the rest of the evenings to myself. I used the time to prepare for my job and for other projects.

The working woman with small children

Of all the women who work outside the home, this woman

has the toughest job of all. Her children cannot dress themselves, and often they are still in diapers. Many of these children
are just learning to feed themselves; some cannot do it at all.
She has to clean them, dress them, feed them, and carry them.
In the morning, she has to pack suitcases in order to make sure
the sitter has everything she might need for the day. Yet in spite
of all this stress, she is expected somehow to keep heart, mind,
and soul intact.

One basic principle applies for the woman in this situation:
the more hectic the schedule, the more important it is to try to
stick to a routine. This working mother needs to carefully plan
exactly what she intends to do from the time she comes home
until the time she goes to bed. Not knowing what to do next only
adds to frustration and keeps her from using her time wisely.

In chapter 10, I will share ideas that can help working
women with their small children. A baby sitter can easily
follow the routine you have established for your infant or
small child. Good habits established early in your children's
lives will make it easier for you to control their behavior and
will help them feel more secure and happy.

Most important, the working woman with small children
must seek the Lord on a daily basis with all her heart, mind, and
soul. Ask Him to help you find control in your life and to see the
things that are truly important for your family. I feel very
strongly that you must have the full weekend for yourself and
your family. You need this time to restore yourself physically
and emotionally. Cleaning worries shouldn't enter your mind
on Sunday.

Hang in there!

I realize that circumstances for each family are different.
Schedules vary. The amount of cooperation from husband
and children varies. Whatever the circumstances, I believe at
least some of these ideas can help every working woman. You
can also use them as a springboard for ideas of your own. The
most important thing is to have a plan. Whether there is one
or one dozen in the family, you need a plan for home cleaning
and organization. Having a plan and sticking to it will give you
more time for the other important things in your life.

The Lord will make your Sabbaths full of joy if you allow Him to. He doesn't want the Sabbath to be a stumbling block at the end of the week to increase your stress. On the contrary, the Sabbath should be an oasis in the desert of your stressful life. You have a whole week to prepare for it. Take full advantage of the time!

What children can do to help you

2 years old
Put toys away

3 years old
Put clothes in hamper
Put clothes in drawers
Start helping to make beds
Clear meal dishes
Empty wastebaskets

5 years old
Get dressed
Fold clothes
Empty dishwasher
Set table
Clean up after pet
Feed pet
Help put groceries away

7 years old
Brush hair
Help straighten drawers and closets
Dust furniture
Vacuum room
Sweep walks
Help in kitchen
Help make school lunch
Schoolwork

8 years old
Brush teeth (Dentists recommend that parents brush their

children's teeth up to this age. At earlier ages, they don't have the dexterity to do a good job.)

Clean bathroom
Clean inside of car
Music lessons
Iron flat items

10 years old
Wash bathroom mirrors
Wash windows
Wash floors in small areas
Polish shoes

Over 10 years old
Wash the car
Mow the lawn
Make dessert
Paint
Clean the refrigerator
Do the yardwork
Iron
Take out the trash
Fix an entire meal
Do the grocery shopping

Chapter 8

Traditions Make Sabbath Special

When I left home to go to college, I took many of my cherished possessions with me. I packed my clothes. I took bedding, small tables, a record player, lamps, and school-related items. I also brought several pictures and keepsakes that held great sentimental value for me. These items would enhance the decor of my dormitory room and remind me of my home, family, and friends.

I arrived on a Sunday. Soon I had unpacked everything and settled into my new dormitory room. Gradually I made new friends and adjusted to the new college routine.

It didn't occur to me at first, but I also did another type of "packing." During the rush of registration, classes, homework assignments, and new activities, these important items remained "packed." But by sunset on Friday, the beginning of my first Sabbath at college, my mind began spontaneously "unpacking" these memories, whether or not I wanted it to. Remembrances of Sabbaths gone by began to flood my thoughts. As I lay on my bed, my eyes filled with tears, and I felt a homesick mixture of joy and sadness. I felt joy because of the many warm memories that were as real as the keepsakes I had used to decorate my room. The sadness came because I couldn't participate in the Sabbath activities of my childhood home.

I could smell the delicious soup that my mother would make every Friday evening. I could hear the hymns coming from the record player. I imagined how the house must look after the final Sabbath-preparation activities. I could picture my family on their knees, praying together and reciting the Lord's Prayer as they welcomed another Sabbath. I would have done anything to be there with them!

My fondest memories of family life revolve around the Sabbath and Sabbath traditions. While in college, I felt closest to my home during the Sabbath. Even now as a married woman and mother, many warm memories unfold during the holy hours—memories of home and church activities, memories of special meals and special friends. Many of those activities involve Sabbath traditions instituted by my parents. As a Seventh-day Adventist young person, these traditions helped to solidify my relationships with my parents, my church, and my God.

Why have Sabbath traditions?

My college experience emphasizes to me the importance of Sabbath traditions. Traditions continue to make the Sabbath special even while we are away from our families. They bring us back home even when we are away from home. They give us security when we are at home. They make every Sabbath special.

Sabbath traditions can make the day special for your children just as they did for me and as I am doing for my family now. The Sabbath will never be meaningful to your children if you don't make an effort to set it apart in their eyes as a special, holy day. If their memories of Sabbath consist only of you frantically trying to "jump start" the family on Saturday morning in order to get them to church, then think what blessings they—and you—will have missed!

Traditions can help teach your children to celebrate the Sabbath when they leave home. I take every avenue to help my children love the Sabbath. I want it to be so ingrained in their minds and hearts that they would feel uncomfortable even to think of not keeping it!

But children can learn only what we teach them. They get their ideas of how to celebrate the Sabbath from you. Of course, how they observe the Sabbath as adults will be their choice, but I want to do all I can to help them decide to follow what they were taught at home.

Beginning with Friday

In your home, talk about and anticipate the Sabbath with joy. When my children ask me—even on Thursdays—why I am cleaning, I answer with a smile, "I'm getting the house ready for Jesus. The Sabbath starts tomorrow evening." Don't talk about the hard work of getting ready for the Sabbath. Instead, talk about the joy and privilege of preparing for the Sabbath. Here are some of the traditions in our house that make the Sabbath special for our family.

The Sabbath bedspread. When I change the beds on Friday morning, I also put out what I call my Sabbath bedspreads. These are the nicest ones I have. My son ran into my bedroom one Friday morning, looked at the bedspread, and exclaimed, "Yeeeah! It's Sabbath today!" He knew what that bedspread meant.

Each bed in the house has a Sabbath bedspread. That way, every child sees a marked difference in his or her bedroom during the holy hours. These bedspreads come off on Sunday morning.

Vacuuming. Vacuuming is almost a daily chore in my home, but it takes on special significance before the Sabbath begins. I always vacuum the whole house just before beginning our other early Sabbath traditions. There's something special about freshly vacuumed carpets to me. It makes the whole house seem that much cleaner.

Setting the mood. On Fridays, the children get their baths around four o'clock in the afternoon, and then they put on their pajamas. I close all the drapes in the house and turn on the lamps in each room. I put on a cassette tape or record of religious music. This sets a relaxed, lovely mood in the home.

Now that my children are older, they enthusiastically go to every room, close drapes, and turn on lamps on their own. They do this even if the sun hasn't set. In the wintertime I will often light candles and oil lamps and put them around the house.

Sabbath toys. As the mood is set, I let the children bring out their special toys that they can play with only on Sabbath.

Since they see these toys only once a week, they think of them as very special. They are quiet toys, such as felts or Bible games. The children also have a large collection of Christian tapes and records. I don't want them to be bored and say that there is nothing to do on the Sabbath. That's why I make sure they have a large variety of toys and music for the Sabbath. On Friday my younger son asked his twin sister, "Aren't you glad that it is almost Sabbath? Soon we'll be able to play with our Sabbath toys!"

As we wait for my husband to come home, I have worship with the children. When my husband comes, the house is dimly lighted, everything is clean, and nice music is playing— soon it will be Sabbath.

Food traditions. I make it a tradition to have soup on Friday nights, just as we did in my childhood home. I usually prepare the soup on Friday morning. Our meal to welcome the Sabbath is always by candlelight. Before the blessing, we discuss what Sabbath means to us and sing, "Sabbath Is a Happy Day." We then offer a prayer to greet the Sabbath.

Several working women have told me that preparing soup for Friday evenings has made coming home from work at the end of the week so much easier. They can relax. I know other women who feed their family spaghetti, salad, and garlic bread on Friday evening. Friday evenings are not a problem for them when they come home from work since they know the spaghetti routine so well.

The busy working woman can use the Friday-evening soup dinner to her advantage. She can serve canned soup in an attractive manner, using her nice bowls and dishes. A candle placed on the table also adds a nice touch. Even though the meal is simple and takes little time to prepare, everyone in the family will feel it is special.

All these traditions are well worth whatever time and effort they cost because they help to prepare my family for a wonderful day, and the children anxiously await it. In fact, my children have encouraged us to add three more traditions to our Sabbath welcome. Along with soup, we now have popcorn and a juice bar on Friday nights. Believe me, they look forward to it. Also, my husband or I read them a story after supper before they go to bed.

The last thing I do when my children go to bed on Friday night is to put their Sabbath clothes in a place where they can see them. We talk about how these clothes are so clean and special because the Lord's day is special.

Here are some Sabbath traditions other women have shared with me. One has fresh flowers in her home every Friday. Another puts a lovely tablecloth on the dining-room table every Friday. One serves blueberry muffins as a Sabbath tradition. Musical families get out the instruments on Friday nights and enjoy making music together. Some families with older children plan a challenging talk on teen life—and take this time to really listen to their teenagers as the kids relate what they are experiencing. Parents share their own experiences and how they are handling their problems. Other families have all kinds of Bible games that they play around the table.

Friday nights can make families closer, especially when there are teens in the home. Spiritual and emotional growth can take place Friday after Friday.

You don't have to spend a lot of money to make the Sabbath special. You don't even need to buy new bedspreads. Instead, think of ways, simple ways, to enhance the Sabbath experience. Just do something that says to your family, "This day is special, and you are special."

Sabbath-morning activities

Plan to get to Sabbath School on time. This helps your children see that Sabbath is special. Why is it that we wouldn't think of being late to work, but it's OK to be late to church? What are we saying to our children? Work is important, but God is not as important? Make sure the family gets to church on time.

You can avoid unnecessary work on the Sabbath and still have the rooms neat and tidy. Many women tell me that their house looks the worst on Sabbath morning. I think it's because they try to sleep in on Sabbath and don't follow the usual routine of making the beds. Get up just as early on Sabbath as any other weekday and follow the morning routine just the same. If the house is going to look in peak condition on any particular day, that day should be the Sabbath.

Sabbath dinner traditions

In our house, we often eat Sabbath dinner at the dining table. At other times, we normally use the dining room only for guests. But since I want to make the day special, I set the dining-room table on Sabbath, and we don't eat in the nook. If your family always uses the main dining room for eating, make this meal special by using nice dishes. Leave the plastic plates and Tupperware cups for meals during the week, and bring out your best for Sabbath. All these little things add to the specialness of the Sabbath. About two years ago, as we sat around the dining-room table for Sabbath dinner, my little girl said, "Today is a very special day. We're eating in the dining room, and we're eating from plates that can break." Even the plates told her that Sabbath was a special day.

Sunday is the day I serve my "big breakfast." We have probably slept in, and I'm in no hurry. We eat leisurely and enjoy being together. On Sundays, we also have an early supper, so we end up with only two meals for that day. I usually try to make the same thing every Sunday for supper so I don't have to think so hard about preparation. For about three months I'll make spaghetti for supper on Sunday. Then for another three months or more, I will make haystacks. Often we go out to eat as a family on this day. Sometimes we just go out for frozen yogurt or ice cream. It's more relaxing when I don't have to worry about what I am going to cook. And these Sunday food traditions also help to enhance our time together as a family.

When your children pack up and go away to college or finally leave your home, what important package of good memories will they take with them? What Sabbath traditions will they take from you to use in their new homes? These things do much more than simply emphasize the importance of Sabbath keeping. They turn the holy hours into a joyful, meaningful celebration—the kind of celebration our Lord originally intended for us to enjoy.

Chapter 9

Help! I'm Having Guests for Sabbath Dinner!

Why do people drop out of the Seventh-day Adventist Church? In an article in the *Adventist Review* ("Where Are Our Missing Members?" 4 May 1989), Monte Sahlin writes:

> In all the surveys and interviews with missing and former Adventists, three out of four "dropouts" indicate that they left for reasons having to do with their relationships with people and groups, while less than one in five left because they no longer believe in some teaching of the church.

It's extremely important that we meet the *social* needs of people if we hope to keep them in the church. People need to feel warmth, acceptance, understanding, and love—particularly those who are new in the faith.

One important way we can reach out to others socially is by sharing our homes and food with them. Sometimes we call this "entertaining." This sounds to me as though we have to put on a show for people, that we must have something wonderful to display to them, or that somehow we have to amuse our guests. I prefer the word *fellowship*. Fellowship means getting together to share ideas and getting to know one another. It's a warm word. When the Lord is in the midst of that kind of fellowship, what a wonderful time of growth and enrichment we can have!

Why don't we invite people home for Sabbath dinner more often? Some are too shy. Some feel their house isn't nice enough or that they don't have fancy things. For some, it's too difficult to get organized for guests on Sabbath. But the main reason for many women I know is that it's too hard to prepare both for the Sabbath *and* for guests. Those who have small children and a house to look after especially feel it is impossible to invite guests to their home on Sabbath.

But if you follow some simple time-saving preparation ideas, you can enjoy having guests at your home on Sabbath. It will add much to your enjoyment of the day and to your children's Sabbath experience as well. No matter how humble the surroundings or how tight the budget, a little planning can make this Sabbath-fellowship experience a delight. Here are some ideas to help minimize the stress of preparing for guests.

Planning early in the week

If everything is planned ahead of time, having guests over need not be a grueling ordeal. Plan your menu so that when shopping day comes, you can pick up everything you need for the meal. You don't have to be a gourmet cook, but whatever you make, you want it to be tasty. A good menu for guests consists of a simple entree, two vegetables, fresh tossed salad, bread or rolls, and a drink. It's easy to put together, and it provides a satisfying meal. Don't make cooking for guests so difficult that you lose interest in doing it. Also, if you make the meal too fancy, your guests may feel they have to "keep up" if they were to invite you to their house. Having guests shouldn't become a competition. It should be a time for enjoying each other's company.

Some women are great bakers. Some are talented dessert makers. I am neither. My desserts are very simple. Sometimes I put two scoops of ice cream in a bowl, and that is dessert. In the summer I often put out a big tray of fresh fruit for dessert. Other times I put berries on top of a slice of pound cake. My desserts are not time-consuming to prepare. Simple, wholesome meals are easier on you and your guests. You can concentrate on enjoying the fellowship rather than on a fancy menu.

I do as much cooking as possible on Wednesday or Thursday evening. Please, *don't* use Friday for cooking! You will be able to enjoy your family so much more on Friday evenings if you aren't so worried about food preparation. Even if you don't have guests, prepare the meal ahead of time for your family.

I prepare the Sabbath entree for guests early in the week. When Friday comes, entrees and desserts are the last things I think about. The hard part is all done by Thursday night! I believe lack of cooking is what makes my Fridays so free. Also, as much as possible, I try to make extra food to put in the freezer for the unexpected times that guests may pop in. Actually, many sauces, entrees, and other dishes often taste better after the passing of time.

You can even prepare the ingredients for the salad on Friday. If you wash the lettuce leaves and then dry them well, they will keep until the next day without wilting or turning brown. (Keep the lettuce in a bowl covered with plastic wrap after cutting it up.) Slice radishes, tomatoes, carrots, and other ingredients. Put each ingredient in a separate sandwich bag, and then keep them in the refrigerator. Tossing the salad when you get back from church takes three minutes. You have saved time on Sabbath by preparing the salad ingredients on Friday.

You can also prepare garlic bread on Friday. Cut the long loaves of French bread in half lengthwise, spread margarine on them, and sprinkle with garlic powder. Put the halves together and then cut them into slices. Place the loaves of French bread back into their bags and put them in the refrigerator. Prior to serving on Sabbath, spread the bread on a cooking sheet and put them in the oven.

If you are preparing fresh vegetables, you can prepare them on Friday too. Wash the vegetables, cut them up into the pot you will cook them in, put a lid on the pot, and put the pot away in the refrigerator.

These Friday food preparations don't take long. The woman working outside the home can do them in the early evening. An older child can do almost all these things on her own.

Setting the table on Friday

Set the table on Friday, early in the afternoon. If you work outside the home, set it in the early evening. Put everything out on the table, including plates, flatware, glasses, napkins, salt shakers, serving dishes, serving spoons, and a centerpiece. This will help you find out if everything will fit on the table without crowding or if you need to use other dishes or arrangements. After putting the serving dishes on the table, remove them and stack them on the kitchen counter somewhere. If you plan exactly what food to put in each dish, everything will be at your fingertips when serving time comes on Sabbath.

Of course, if you don't have a separate dining area, it's impractical to set the table on Friday. Still, you can stack the plates, flatware, napkins, and glasses in a corner somewhere close to the dinner table so that everything is close at hand. As soon as breakfast is over on Sabbath morning, put the table-cloth on the table. If there are older kids in the home, they can set the table. Now you don't have to worry about setting the table after church!

My children get excited when I set the dining-room table on Friday. They want to know who is coming for Sabbath dinner. After telling them who our guests will be, I talk with them about the things we can do to make our friends feel welcome. If other children are coming, we talk about sharing toys and not fighting with someone who might be playing with a favorite toy. Teenagers often enjoy inviting their friends home for Sabbath. It can help keep them from getting bored during the Sabbath hours. It's always more fun for a teen to have a friend around—and not just his parents. Also, you can make sure that the kids are observing the Sabbath appropriately if they are with you.

Sabbath duties

Before leaving for church, set the oven timer and put the entree in the oven. "What if you don't have an oven timer?" Here are three ideas.

You can divide the oven time into two equal parts. If the recipe calls for one hour at 350 degrees, do the first thirty minutes at 350 degrees before leaving for church. Do the second thirty minutes after returning from church. By the time the second thirty minutes of cooking are complete, you will have finished preparing everything else. Be sure to turn the oven off before going to church!

A second idea is to leave the entree dish in the oven at a lower temperature. Adjust the temperature of the oven to 150 or 200 degrees. Cover the dish with foil. When you return from church, the cooking should be done or almost done. And the aroma in the house is so good!

Or you can cook the entree completely before going to church. After cooking, turn the oven off, cover the dish, and leave it in the oven. Upon returning from church, turn the oven to 250 degrees. The entree will be heated by the time you're ready to serve.

Once you are back home from church, your husband can help change the kids' clothes. If pressured for time, don't change their clothes. Put on an apron and check the entree. Get the salad fixings out of the refrigerator and toss everything together. Put the salad bowl back in the refrigerator. Now make the drink. After the drink is made, bring out the vegetable pot and start steaming the vegetables. Warm up the rolls now too. As you're doing these things, look around the kitchen and pick up anything that is out of place. Put the few dishes that were recently dirtied in the dishwasher. Straighten up all around. Dump cans and kitchen paper. Leaving things out just makes cleaning up more difficult later.

When your guests arrive, you can greet them calmly because you have everything under control. The meal is ready, and the kitchen is in reasonable order.

Now get out the serving dishes, start putting food in them, and put the food on the table. When everything is on the table, serve the children. I serve my children before I call anyone to the table; it makes for a much smoother beginning. Then call the guests and seat them around the table. Now sit down, relax, and enjoy the meal!

Planning ahead for Sabbath dinner can make all the difference. Sabbath dinner will be much less of a burden if you follow some or all of these ideas.

Setting a pretty table inexpensively

Many women feel that they don't have pretty things with which to decorate the dinner table. Maybe they don't have any china or stoneware. Crystal is out of the question for many. The only kind of tablecloth some have are the plastic ones. Actually, you don't have to have fancy or beautiful things to set a lovely table. Try to be creative with color; it can make a real difference.

I believe that every home should have a set of plain white- or bone-colored plates. The neutral color will allow you to vary the place settings by using different tablecloths and napkins. I got a set of bone-colored stoneware dishes for ten dollars at a discount store about eight years ago. I have used them repeatedly to set a lovely table.

You can get nice, inexpensive dishes if you keep your eyes open. I am always on the lookout. I check local stores, discount stores, and secondhand stores—and often find inexpensive dishes that look very nice on the table, yet don't cost too much. One tip: Don't buy anything that has less than six place settings.

I strongly encourage women to buy one bone or white lace tablecloth. Look for them at sales or in secondhand stores. You can even use bed sheets for tablecloths. I do. They look lovely and allow me a wide variety of choices for color. Don't cut them; let them flow gracefully to the ground. Sometimes I place a lace tablecloth on top of a sheet for a really nice effect. If you have sewing talents, you can make matching napkins and place mats out of the sheets. Set the table using napkins of two different colors sometimes. If youhave an even number of people, alternate peach-colored napkins with cream-colored ones. The same thing can be done with place mats. Also, you can mix peach-colored place mats with cream-colored napkins and vice versa. With a little creativity, you can set a beautiful table inexpensively.

Many women do not have matching serving dishes. Only my nice set of dishes has matching serving pieces. I took care of this problem by looking for sales on Pyrex bowls at the local discount store. I bought some with lids and some without, some large and some small. They look like a set because they are all Pyrex. I have a glass pitcher, and I put out my clear glasses. I can use these serving dishes with stoneware, china, or anything.

Those unexpected guests

I try to be prepared all the time for unexpected guests. More than once, friends have shown up at our door right before a meal!

Here is a list of foods that can be easily prepared on short notice. Keep them in the house in case friends drop by unexpectedly.

Canned or bottled spaghetti sauce

Spaghetti

Frozen mixed vegetables

Instant mashed potatoes

Cans of beans—any variety

Cans of instant "heat and serve" soup

Boxes of fancy crackers

Any kind of cake mix

Any type of canned pie filling (berries are best) to put on the cake

If you keep these things on hand, you won't worry when unexpected guests arrive. You'll be ready!

Finally, the fellowship

In all your preparations, don't leave out wonderful Christian fellowship. Don't lose the opportunity to show people you care because it may seem too hard to prepare the dinner or because your dishes aren't nice enough.

It's wonderful to invite your close friends or those you admire and respect to your home. But there are many others who need your fellowship. Those who feel left out, who cannot afford to feed you in return, who are not popular, who never get asked out. You know who they are. They go to your church, and your care will keep them in church. They live in your neighborhood; your care will draw them to your church and open their eyes to the Saviour.

These are guests whom it will lay on you no great burden to receive. You will not need to provide for them elaborate or expensive entertainment. You will need to make no effort at display. The warmth of a genial welcome, a place at your fireside, a seat at your home table, the privilege of sharing the blessing of the hour of prayer, would to many of these be like a glimpse of heaven (Ellen G. White, *The Adventist Home*, p. 448).

Remember, too, the words of Jesus, "When thou makest a dinner or a supper, call not thy friends, . . . nor thy rich neighbours; lest they also bid thee again, and a recompense be made thee. But when thou makest a feast, call the poor, the maimed, the lame, the blind: And thou shalt be blessed; for they cannot recompense thee: for thou shalt be recompensed at the resurrection of the just" (Luke 14:12-14).

Chapter 10

What About the Children?

You may not think that a chapter about children fits in a book about Sabbath preparation. As women know, however, children are a major factor in home organization. I would do an injustice to both career women and women who spend their full time at home if I didn't tell you how to work with your children to make the most of your home-management plan. You can't keep up with your home systematically if you haven't instilled order in your children's lives.

In previous chapters, I have explained my Sabbath-preparation plan in detail, but how do these details help women with small babies who cry throughout the night and who want to be fed at all hours? How will a woman have the strength to do anything in a planned fashion if she is exhausted? How can she wake up early for devotions if she has been up three or four times during the night?

For women with infants, life can become a vicious cycle. You try to follow a program for your home. Your children won't let you because they demand your attention constantly. You try it again the next day, but it seems the more you attempt to organize your life, the more demanding the children become. Is there any hope for you, the mother of young children? Yes, there is!

Order and the infant
The secret to coping with home management when you have

babies at home is to instill a sense of order in your children from the very beginning.

> The cultivation of order and taste is an important part of the education of children. . . .
>
> As the guardian and teacher of your children, you are in duty bound to do every little thing in the home with nicety and in order. . . .
>
> Remember that in heaven there is no disorder, and that your home should be a heaven here below. . . .
>
> If your habits are correct, if you reveal neatness and order, virtue and righteousness, sanctification of soul, body, and spirit, you respond to the words of the Redeemer, "Ye are the light of the world" (Ellen G. White, *Child Guidance*, p. 110).

> With his manifold devices Satan begins to work with their [children's] tempers and their wills as soon as they are born. Their safety depends upon the wisdom and the vigilant care of the parents. They must strive in the love and fear of God to preoccupy the garden of the heart, sowing the good seeds of a right spirit, correct habits, and the love and fear of God (Ellen G. White, *The Adventist Home*, p. 202).

The benefits of routine

Such appeals for careful training of our infants sound wonderful, and the arrival of a new little one is a high point for a young couple. But little do they know of the chaos that can rapidly set in when a baby comes to live with them! The baby cries, sleeps, and eats at any time of the day or night. The mother becomes tired and irritable. The husband wonders where he fits in this new triangle. Now his meals are never ready, his clothes are not clean, and he hardly speaks to his wife. When he comes home, the place looks like a tornado hit it, and, often, both mother and child are crying. Most of us accept these circumstances as unavoidable; we believe there are no options. I strongly believe there is a better way, a more orderly and happy way.

I believe you can be a rested mother and at the same time keep up with all your responsibilities. I don't say this because I have been a super mother but because I have had a routine to follow every day. A routine, faithfully followed, will give you time for household duties and for your child. Your husband won't feel uncared for. Meals will be on time, and the clothes will be clean. You will also have some time every day for yourself and to grow in your life together as husband and wife. Sound too good to be true? From my own experience, I know a routine can help you organize your life when you have infants. The alternative is the chaos most of us have come to accept as inevitable.

Families with infants need to plan for bedtimes, nap times, waking times, bath times, and feeding times. A typical routine for the baby might go something like this:

6:30 a.m.—Wake up and first feeding.
7:15 a.m.—Nap time.
9:00 a.m.—Wake up, play, go for a walk.
10:00 a.m.—Bath time.
10:30 a.m.—Second feeding.
11:00 a.m.—Middle-of-day nap.
2:30 p.m.—Wake up and third feeding.
3:00 p.m.—Wake time.
5:30 p.m.—Prepare for bed.
6:00 p.m.—Fourth feeding.
6:30 p.m.—To bed for the night.
10:00 p.m.—Fifth feeding.

You will probably need to add an additional feeding around two o'clock in the morning for a while, but after a few weeks this should no longer be necessary. The ten o'clock feeding in the evening should also be unnecessary after eight weeks or so. When your baby is two months old, he or she may well be sleeping from six-thirty in the evening until six-thirty in the morning with no interruptions.

Here are two other pluses that come from a routine.

Security. Your children will know that they will be taken care of. You remove from them—even as infants—the responsibility for determining when they should sleep and eat. Very early on, they learn that you will supply their needs at the same time every day. Children thrive on regularity. They like to sense the boundaries. This gives them security.

Health. When children don't eat between meals, they have healthy appetites at mealtime and healthy teeth. Flu and cold epidemics will touch them less often because they get enough sleep at night, they eat at good intervals, and they drink plenty of water.

These early years of order and regularity will also lay the foundation for future benefits. As your children grow older, they will feel a sense of love and security, but they will also know that the world does not revolve around them to give them their every wish and whim. As they go to school or work, they will bring patience and order into their efforts.

Our tasks as homemakers are not easy. With working women, the task is doubly hard. A system of order for the child of a working woman is doubly important.

My views on regularity in the lives of infants and small children may not be for everyone. That's perfectly fine. But I am convinced it can make a difference in your children's lives and in your home. Remember, it's your responsibility to develop good habits of order and spiritual values in your children so that they may develop like Jesus, who "increased in wisdom and stature, and in favour with God and man" (Luke 2:52).

Chapter 11

Completing the Cleaning

In this chapter we will go beyond the weekly ritual of cleaning for Sabbath. We will go where few dare to go. Come with me as we travel to the farthest corner of the closet, to the back of the drawers, beneath the beds, and under the tables. We're now ready to complete the cleaning of the house.

Sure, it sounds like a lot of work, but don't worry! A plan will make the job much easier. A good plan will allow you to work as fast or as slow as your schedule allows. You might do this cleaning and organizing all at one time, or you could do it on Sundays or for a few hours a week.

First, let's talk about important papers.

Important document organization

Here's how we do it at our house. On top of our desk sits a small file rack containing five different-colored file folders. These are labeled as follows:

1. House/car payment books
2. Bank statements
3. Bills to pay
4. Receipts to be filed
5. Income tax papers

The top drawer of the desk contains pens, pencils, markers, transparent tape, a stapler, and scissors. A side drawer has envelopes, stamps, paper, and an address book. When it's time to pay the bills, everything is at our fingertips. At tax time, we grab the income-tax folder, where we keep all the tax forms and tax-related receipts.

We pay bills once a month. You may prefer to pay more often. Whatever the time frame, a system will always help. When it's time to pay bills, we grab the "Bills to pay" folder and start opening all the bills in the folder. Paying bills isn't fun, but this simple system makes the whole thing more tolerable.

We also maintain a larger general file. Each manila folder in the file is labeled by month and year. We file all receipts for the month in the appropriate folder. Each set of folders for the year is kept for five years, just in case of an audit by the Internal Revenue Service. Behind these monthly files, we keep folders with other important documents (insurance, warranties, instruction manuals, etc.). You may want to keep very valuable documents in a locked fireproof box or even in a bank safe deposit box. With our system, simple as it is, we never have a problem finding an important paper.

Mail organization

Mail can overwhelm you if you don't have a plan for taking care of it. Here is what I do.

When the mail comes, I sort it—immediately dumping all the junk mail. The bills go directly into the "Bills to pay" file folder. I keep everything addressed to my husband that I think he may be remotely interested in. What may seem like junk mail to me may be of great importance to him. I put all his mail in a pile on his dining-room chair. When he comes home, he looks through it, dumping what he doesn't want and putting away the rest of it. After I have sorted my husband's mail, I sit down and enjoy my mail. I love getting letters from friends—and writing them. I have a "stationery box," a plastic filing box that contains stationery for all occasions—birthday cards, anniversary cards, get-well-soon cards, thank-you cards, and so on. I also keep pens, stamps, and an address book in the box. Everything is in one place. If there is time, I answer letters right away. If not, I file the letter in the box and come back to it later.

I like to be near the calendar when I sort the mail. I use a calendar with large squares to record important appointments, weddings, parties, dinner invitations, etc. In the appropriate square, I write down the occasion, who has invited us, the time, the place, and the phone number if needed. Now I can discard the invitation after recording this information on the calendar. I keep the calendar by the kitchen telephone, with pens and pencils close by.

I also use the calendar to remind me of deadlines. You can use the calendar to remind you of all the things you need to do during the week. Or you may want to have *two* calendars—one for home organization and another for appointments. I am a believer in calendars, the bigger the better.

Drawer organization

Most discount stores carry small plastic baskets, usually in three sizes. I use these to organize my drawers. The middle size fits inside our chest of drawers. For the children, I put three of the baskets in one drawer. They put their underpants, T-shirts, and socks in separate baskets. I do the same with my underwear drawer. The baskets keep all the garments in place and prevent the clothing from sliding around and getting mixed up. They also help the children put the clothing in the proper places. Don't store everything in the chest of drawers—only clothing. Find another place to put the glue, the mail, and the marbles.

After you've straightened and cleaned the drawers, put a bar of strong-smelling deodorant soap in each drawer. Your clothes will smell fresh and clean.

Here is an organizing system that works well for me, not only for closets but also for organizing drawers, cupboards, kitchens, garages, etc.

You'll need several large trash bags and some empty, sturdy, large boxes. If possible, get boxes that are all the same size and have lids. Finally, a pack of 3 x 5 cards completes your list of necessary items.

For closets, decide whether to start with the shelves or the clothing. Then take your three bags and label them: (1) "throw away," (2) "give away," and (3) "put away." Each item will go in one of the three bags. When sorting garments in the closet, decide which to leave hanging and then place the other garments in one of the three bags. Clothes that you haven't worn for three or more years, you should put in the "throw-away" or "give-away" bag. Put the clothes that are in bad shape in the "throw-away" bag. Clothes in good condition go in the "give away" bag. Certain outfits or other items that have sentimental value but no current practical use go in the "put-away" bag. Also use the "put-away" bag for items that you can use but that don't belong in the closet.

Don't let sentiment get the best of you when sorting the closet. That eighth-grade graduation dress that is now five sizes too small should be thrown or given away—unless your great-great-grandmother made it by hand and your two-year-old daughter is looking forward to wearing it to her eighth-grade graduation! Sometimes it takes a friend to help you decide not to keep things. When a friend asked me to help her go through her things, we discarded many items that she wouldn't have gotten rid of on her own. When I left, she said, "Thank you for letting me keep *some* things."

Now that you have cleaned the closet and sorted the things in it, it's time to put back in the closet the items you will keep. I organize the closet by hanging all my dressy clothes on the left side. I arrange them by colors, keeping garments of similar color together. From left to right, I hang my suits, blouses, and skirts. I keep the dresses and blouses I use for home wear on the right side of the closet. Next to these, I hang my dress pants on thick hangers. The thick hangers help to prevent creases. My bathrobes go farthest to the right.

I organize my husband's closet by hanging his dress suits on the left side of the closet on suit hangers. Following these to the right are the dress shirts, the slacks he wears to work, the shirts he wears to work, and his bathrobe. A tie rack hangs next to his bathrobe. This serves as a partition between dress clothing and casual clothing. His casual shirts are in the far-right side of the closet. His sweaters lie on the top shelf of the closet, folded and stacked one on top of the other.

We both have shoe racks on the floor of the closet. That's where we also keep a sturdy box filled with shoe-shine equipment. I store my dress shoes in plastic shoe boxes purchased from a discount store, and if I have a matching purse, I place it on top of the corresponding box. I keep my casual shoes (sandals, flats, tennis shoes, etc.) in the shoe rack for easy access. I store my belts in the same type of plastic boxes I use for my shoes. Belt racks also work very well.

Now stand back and admire your closet. Not only is it organized, it's also clean and contains only necessary items.

Probably by now, your three bags are full. So take the "throw-away" bag and throw it away! Put the "give-away" bag in the garage. Wait until you've collected the "give-away" bags from all your closets, then call the Salvation Army, the Dorcas Society, or any other favorite charity and have them take the bags. What about the "put-away" bags? Let start working on these.

The storage plan

Now take out those boxes with the lids, the 3 x 5 cards, a pen, and a marker. With the marker, write 1 on the front side of the first box. Then number the other boxes in succession. Write 1 on the top of a 3 x 5 card and then number the other cards in succession. As you place items from the "put-away" bag into each of the numbered boxes, record each item on a corresponding card. At the bottom of each card, write the location of the box—for example, "top basement shelf, right side." Then store the cards in a 3 x 5 card file box. Continue cleaning and sorting items in each room of the house.

How long will this take? That depends on the state the house is in at the time. With small children at home, it could take between three and seven weeks or more. You can work at this while the children are down for naps or after they are in bed for the night. If your children are happy and close by, you can do it while they play. Don't give up! Keep working at it! It feels so good when the job is done! The system is so simple to set up, and it is easy to use once it is in place. You'll love it!

Kitchen organization

By this time, you should be feeling good about your organized rooms and closets. But now the time has come to deal with the kitchen. Get out the bags, the boxes, the file cards, the pen, and the marker again. The same storage system works here. You probably have pots and mixers in your kitchen drawers that you rarely use and that are taking up space. The storage plan will help you solve this problem.

Decide how much time you will devote to the kitchen. Then set a goal for that block of time. For instance, if you have an hour to work on the kitchen, you might set a goal to organize two groups of cupboard shelves. If you have several hours, you might organize half the cupboards in the kitchen. Kitchen organization won't seem so frustrating if you set intermediate goals and meet them.

Some items useful for organizing kitchen drawers and cupboards are flatware dividers, flat baskets, and Lazy Susans. The Lazy Susans work well in the cupboards for storing canned goods, condiments, and other similar items; they make items easy to reach.

The large bottom shelf of one of the lower cupboards is often a good place to store the big pots and pans with their lids. I find it helpful to store baking dishes and pans together. Keep everyday dishes close at hand in the bottom shelf of one of the cupboards. Store glasses according to frequency of use. Put the rarely used ones on top shelves and the everyday ones on a lower shelf. Store serving dishes together. Put the nicer plates on higher shelves since they are not used as much. Put the Tupperware all together in one place—large containers on one side, medium-sized containers in the middle, and smaller pieces on the other side of the shelf.

Keep two sets of flatware dividers in the flatware drawer—one for everyday flatware, the second for the nicer set. Narrower flatware dividers work well for ice-cream scoops, salad tongs, and serving spoons. Keep cooking utensils—spatulas, wooden and plastic spoons, eggbeaters, ladles, etc.—in a bucket next to the stove. Cookbooks and recipes go above the stove. Don't forget to set aside one drawer for foil paper, plastic film, and plastic bags.

You'll find it's convenient to have the spices and condiments in the cupboard next to the stove. This will cut down on walking back and forth to get them when you cook. If you put aluminum foil on the bottom and even on the racks of the oven, you'll decrease the times that you will have to clean the oven. Putting foil on all your cookie sheets will make cleaning them easy too.

COMPLETING THE CLEANING 109

Try to keep counters clear. You need as much counter space as possible. As you clean the kitchen, think about what makes sense. Does it make sense to keep hot pads far from the stove? Items used frequently should be kept nearby; items used less frequently should be kept farther away.

Now that you've finished with the kitchen, go out and celebrate! You have completed the cleaning!

Certain cleaning jobs need to be done only infrequently. I like to schedule these jobs on one of the calendars. Here are some suggestions for how frequently to do certain types of cleaning.

Quarterly. Wash windows.

Semiannually. Vacuum under all furniture, bring out and put away seasonal clothing.

Annually. Clean drapes and rugs, can and freeze, indoor painting.

Now, get to work! "She looketh well to the ways of her household, and eateth not the bread of idleness" (Proverbs 31:27).

Chapter 12

Setting the Home Atmosphere

For the past eleven chapters, we've covered the practical business of homemaking and how to do it efficiently. But your happiness and success as a homemaker depend on much more than just a few good ideas. An efficient schedule may be the effective tool that helps you to be ready for the Sabbath on time, but ultimately, by itself, it won't bring contentment—either to you or to your family members.

What will make the difference? What can make your home the "heaven on earth" that you want it to be? I believe your happiness and the happiness of your family rest heavily on the attitudes you have about your life as a homemaker.

The influence of a mother

As mother, wife, and homemaker, you do an extremely important job. "The king upon his throne has no higher work than has the mother," Ellen White writes. "The mother is queen of her household. She has in her power the molding of her children's characters, that they may be fitted for the higher, immortal life. An angel could not ask for a higher mission; for in doing this work she is doing service for God" (*The Adventist Home*, p. 231).

I like the illustration of mother as "queen." To be a queen is a high office, a position that carries considerable influence. The mother as "queen" of the home has an infinitely profound influence on the members of her family. She is like a thermostat; she sets the spiritual and emotional temperature of the home.

I offer as evidence a family my husband and I have known for several years. We are quite good friends. They are a family of five, and we are a family of five, but that is where the similarity ends. My friend, the mother of that family, is a softspoken, almost timid, young woman. She seldom raises her voice. When looking for her children, she won't even raise her voice to call them! Instead, she goes from room to room looking for them. Her family is just like her in this respect. The children and husband sit quietly for their meals; they are generally soft spoken. They are a happy, *quiet* family.

On the other hand, my family is quite the opposite. I don't have a whispering type of voice. When I look for family members, I yell!

I get excited and loud when I'm happy. I also love to talk. My children also get loud when they're happy. When we sit down at the supper table, we become a *noisy*, happy family.

Each family reflects the personality of the mother.

Mothers can also have a negative impact on the feeling of the home. A depressed mother can twist the thermostat dial downward. Insecurity and confusion in the mother will haunt the family. A moody woman removes the sense of security family members need. No one knows when she will scream or when she will kiss and hug. Sure, some children have strong personalities that will withstand these conditions, but they are the exception, not the rule.

If you want a spirit of love and peace at home, it needs to start with you. The apostle Peter says that the best adornment for a woman is a meek and gentle spirit (see 1 Peter 3). This is the spirit that should reign in our homes.

But this is certainly easier said than done. How do we develop that attitude? Read on!

Developing a pleasant home atmosphere

Here are several suggestions for setting the proper mood at home. I credit the book, *The Bride's Book of Ideas: A Guide to Christian Homemaking*, by Margaret Palmer and Ethel

Browman (Wheaton Ill.: Tyndale House Publishers, 1975), for some of these suggestions.

1. Be content with what you have. It's so easy to forget. Unwittingly, you fall into the rut of keeping up with the Joneses—after all, that's what society stresses. Without thinking, you start comparing what you have—your home, your college degrees, your cars—with those of everyone around you. As a result, you may get depressed. You may feel that the good things of life have passed you by.

What's happening? As soon as you make "me" the focus of your life, you become selfish and then miserable. You forget that it's the Lord who has given each person different talents. To some, God has given material wealth, but He holds these individuals responsible for the use of these means. Whatever your situation, accept God's purposes and be content with what you have.

If you go into debt trying to buy a lot of material goods, it becomes hard to survive, let alone be happy. A financial burden doesn't help the marriage, and it can sour the atmosphere of the home.

During our first year of marriage, Tom and I lived in a tiny apartment. It was so small, I could stand in the middle of it and clean the whole house! It seemed to me that all my brothers and sisters had started off their married lives much better than I had. They all had lovely apartments and furniture. I looked at my friends and felt they, too, were better off than I was. While I was feeling sorry for myself, I remembered Philippians 4:11: "I have learned, in whatsoever state I am, therewith to be content."

I stopped comparing my material possessions with those of others. I thought of my wonderful husband, who was committed to me and our marriage. I had a roof over my head and all that I needed to set up house. Most important, Tom and I had established a home with Christ as the center. We had something of even greater value than the most expensive furniture or apartment. It's been fun starting from scratch and building from there. Over the years, we have avoided trying to keep up with the Joneses. What a waste of energy and finances that would have been!

2. Be happy with your situation. This is similar to the previous guideline but not exactly the same. Learn to be content with not only your level of wealth but also with your circumstances. Learn to be happy whatever your job may be, wherever you live, whatever your marital status, whether or not you have children. Lack of contentment will affect your family.

Those who are single might feel you are off the hook because you live alone and are not responsible for anyone's attitudes but your own. Not so! You still have an influence on your friends and on those who work with you. If you decide to pout and be bitter, you will poison your relationships with others. Next, you'll start blaming the Lord for how unfair life is. In actuality, none of us have anyone to blame but ourselves for our attitudes.

You may not have all the answers to your problems, but one thing is for sure. You control your attitude. Nobody can make you miserable unless you choose to be miserable.

Just this morning, my little girl dropped the Lego house that she had lovingly made. She started crying, and with good reason. All her work was spoiled. I wanted to see if I could get her to change her attitude. I said, "Instead of letting Satan make you mad, sad, and depressed, why don't you make a better house?" She stopped crying, and a tiny smile formed on her face. In an hour she called me and showed me her new house, which was bigger and prettier than the first one. I applauded her and said, "See what can happen when you decide to have a happier attitude? Not only that, you didn't let Satan make you sad."

3. Treat your husband with courtesy and expect the same treatment from him. Few things are as unattractive as a woman belittling her husband or scolding him as if he were a child. Treat your husband as you want to be treated. How many of us want to be belittled by our husbands?

Sometimes in your anger or frustration, you may forget to be courteous and understanding. Some have husbands with wonderful dispositions, who are always willing to please. Don't use those attributes to get what you want. Don't become demanding just because your husband won't retaliate. You want to have an attractive atmosphere for your husband. You don't want to give him a reason to stay late at the workplace or to dread coming home. Treat your husband as a king, and he'll want to treat you as queen. All this plays an important part in developing a pleasant home atmosphere.

4. *Remember that the husband is the head of the house.* Some wives may deal harshly and impatiently with their husbands because they feel they make better decisions. This may be true, but you need to be careful not to remove your husband from his rightful, God-given position in the home.

My husband always gives me the opportunity to voice my opinions and concerns. He never makes an important decision without consulting me. But he has the last word in our home. If husbands and wives work together and pray together, the decisions they make will be from the Lord.

Too often, when the wife dominates in the home, the husband is left frustrated and resentful and the children become confused. Your influence will have greater impact if your husband and children sense your support for the husband as head of the house.

5. *Thank the Lord for the children.* During hard, hectic days, the children seem to get in your way. Their crying, their runny noses, and their silly arguments can make you irritable. But an attitude of gratitude can temper your impatient spirit. Children are a gift from God. They are bone of your bone, flesh of your flesh, mirrors of yourself. "Lo, children are an heritage of the Lord: and the fruit of the womb is his reward" (Psalm 127:3).

If you see your children as stumbling blocks, you have already become too selfish. It's easy to become pleasers of ourselves, with hearts that have become too hard to care for anyone else. Children help protect us from this attitude. "The sympathy, forbearance, and love required in dealing with children would be a blessing in any household. . . . The presence of a child in a home sweetens and refines. A child brought up in the fear of the Lord is a blessing" (Ellen G. White, *The Adventist Home*, p. 160).

6. *Give the Lord His rightful place.* When you completely give your life to the Lord and allow Him to be the center of your home, He will control your home and your attitudes. Jesus says in John 15:5, "Without me ye can do nothing." All your best

intentions will fail unless you give the Lord absolute sway in your life.

Your home can be a place where joy and peace will abide. It can be a home where the Lord loves to dwell. People you know will covet the atmosphere of love and peace that engulfs it. Following these six steps, especially this last one, will make your home a blessing to your family and to everyone who comes under its influence. You can effectively adjust the "thermostat" of your home for the glory of God and the benefit of all.

A few final words about discipline

Something you have never done before will seem hard to do initially. Once it becomes a habit, however, it will seem easy. You have a choice to make. You can decide not to try the ideas we have talked about in this book, or you can put forth some effort. The effort requires discipline—self-discipline.

Some people have a knack for self-discipline. Others have a more difficult time. Most of us, including myself, are disciplined in some areas and not so well disciplined in others. It will take some measure of discipline to have the house in good order by the Sabbath. It will take some discipline to maintain a devotional experience. It will take some discipline to tidy up the night before. It will take some discipline to wash, dry, fold, and put away the laundry.

Acquiring new habits may not seem like fun. But it's fun to live in a well-ordered home, with a content family. It's fun to have fellowship with others in your home, especially with a minimum of stressful preparation. It's fun to receive the Sabbath with a sense of joy, peace, and rest. And the process of reaching these goals also becomes fun as you put forth the effort to try new ideas.

Out of a misplaced sense of what is important, some women spend hours doing certain types of work that aren't too important. Certainly this shows discipline, but this type of discipline is meaningless and soon turns into drudgery. As you apply the ideas in this book to your home, you will find, as have many other women, that the drudgery will be eased. The small amount of discipline you need to try these ideas will save you time, not make more work for you.

Yes, it may take a determination that you may not find within yourself to maintain an orderly home, but the Lord can provide that determination. Through faith and prayer, you can have the same assurance Paul had: "I can do all things through Christ which strengtheneth me" (Philippians 4:13).

Chapter 13

Yara Answers Your Questions

In this last chapter, I want to answer the questions that most frequently come up at my seminars or in other settings when I talk about home management. In these questions that other women have asked, you'll probably see questions that you have too. I hope the answers will be helpful.

Question: I would like to pick up the night before as you suggest. What if my husband doesn't cooperate with me?

Answer: I wish I had a simple answer to this one, but I don't. The first few weeks of marriage are ideal for asking husbands to help because at that time they are willing to do almost anything, even jump off a cliff, for their brides!

If your husband has gone for years without showing any interest in helping with the home, it is unlikely that he will begin to do so now. You can't always change your spouse. I would tell him about the ideas you have learned for organizing the home and ask nicely for his cooperation. If this doesn't bring about results, demanding, nagging, or whining will be even less effective.

You must decide what is important to you. Unfortunately, if you want a neat, orderly home, you may have to pick up after your husband. If you're not willing to do that, then you will need to be content with a less-orderly house.

Question: I'm not a working mother, but I am very busy with home schooling my children. What would you suggest for me?

Answer: It all depends on the ages and grade levels of your children and your philosophy of home schooling. If you are teaching young children during the morning hours, you wouldn't need to change much of the daily schedule I've suggested. You can care for the early-morning activities and still be ready to teach by nine o'clock. On Thursdays, make Sabbath cleaning part of your children's education.

If your children are junior high or high-school age, they can help clean the house in the mornings before schooling begins.

If your schedule for home schooling requires more time, then I recommend you follow the plan for working women. For best results, maintain a consistent, daily pattern.

Question: It takes me a long time to cook because I make everything from scratch. Any ideas?

Answer: I recommend that you not change your menus too often. Keep the same basic menus for several weeks. This way you can make sauces, bread, granola, spreads, beans, etc., in large quantities, freeze them, and then thaw them as needed.

If you must have everything fresh, put your entree ingredients together the night before the meal. Then the only thing you will need to do the next day is to put the entree in the oven.

Question: How much ironing do you do?

Answer: Very little. I am particular about how I wash my husband's shirts. They never sit in the dryer. I always get them out before the dryer stops and hang them up *immediately.* If I do this systematically, I never have to iron a shirt. I deal with all our dress-up clothes the same way. For my kids' daily clothes, I fold them immediately after drying, and they never look wrinkled.

Question: Has there ever been a time when your house got messy?

Answer: You bet! Not only that, there are times when my house becomes totally messy. We're a normal family, and I have normal kids. The difference is that when my house gets messy,

I have a plan of action. I know where and how to start. I can have the house picked up in no time. A home organization plan will make it possible for you to do the same.

Question: I want to thoroughly clean my home because it is such a mess. Where do I begin?

Answer: I would begin in the room that people most often see. This is usually the living room. Concentrate on that room, following the complete cleanup plan in chapter 11. Plan for a time every day, every other day, or weekly to devote to cleaning that room. The evening, after the children are in bed, is a good time. It may even be worth it to have a baby sitter watch the children once or twice a week to give you time to clean.

After thoroughly cleaning the living room, do the family room, the bedrooms, the bathrooms, and the kitchen—in that order. The last area to attack should be the garage. It may take you many weeks to get the house really clean and organized, but it will be worth it. Remember, as you finish one room, you must tidy it up every night, or you will be back to square one.

Working women can use the same system, but it will take longer. Also, the working woman may have to forego her free Sundays until the work is done.

Question: My home looks worse on the Sabbath than on any other day. What can I do?

Answer: I think the problem stems from sleeping in on Sabbath morning. Somehow we feel that we don't need to get up as early on Sabbath as we do during the rest of the week. I don't agree with this. I get up just as early on Sabbath, and so do my children. I follow the same morning routine. When we leave our home for church, our house is completely clean—just as it was Friday night.

Question: How can I help guests feel comfortable while they are staying in my home for several days?

Answer: You can do several things to add a nice touch. Place a letter addressed to your guests in the guest room, where they can see it as they walk in. In it, tell them how happy you are to have them in your home. That makes the welcome special.

Set a pitcher of cold water and cups in the room for their use. A basket of fresh fruit and crackers is also a nice treat.

Supply the guest room with good books and magazines to read.

Let them use one of your alarm clocks.

If guests spend three or more nights at my home, I empty out the drawers in their room for their use. I take their suitcases to the garage or family room so that they can be comfortable and not have suitcases crowd them. I give them the drawers in the bathroom too.

I always let guests use the hamper in their room.

All these things add an extra touch of care, and your guests will enjoy it.

Question: Schedules, routines, and the like go against my personality. A weekly schedule binds me, and I don't like feeling bound. What do you suggest for people like me?

Answer: I think that free-spirited people are great. But I have observed that women with this kind of personality often have the most disorganized homes—not because they are messy or dirty people but because their free spirit moves them to do something other than clean. They are often distracted as they try to get ready for the Sabbath.

If you really want to be truly free, you need to find a system of home maintenance that gives the time to do what you want. If you could be done with housework by nine o'clock in the morning, you'd be free to do as you please the rest of the day. Wouldn't that be worth some organization and routine? Most important, your mind will be free too. You won't have your messy house in the back of your mind all the time.

A system to follow will give the free-spirited woman the time to be truly free and spontaneous.

Question: My home is very small, and the small size makes it hard to be organized. What do you suggest?

Answer: My first suggestion is to go through the complete cleanup plan very thoroughly with the help of a friend. If you are a person who keeps *everything*, a friend can help you get rid of things that you haven't had the heart to give away.

If you still have a house full of things you seldom use, you might look into public mini-storage units. The rental charge on these is minimal, and you can store all those Christmas decorations, desks, dressers, and miscellaneous items to make more room for the things that you need.

Remember also that dark woods, drapes, and heavy furniture make a room look smaller. So does excessive use of plants. Essential furniture, placed nicely in a room, looks better than many beautiful pieces crowded into a small room.

Question: I have a hard time trying to decide what my homemaking priorities are. How can I set them straight?

Answer: Perhaps chapter 1 will help you in this area. Think what would make you feel successful as a homemaker and then determine if these same things will help you as a Christian woman. This will help you develop a good perspective. Listen to your family and see if you are meeting their needs. The family should be high on your priority list.

Of course, nothing can take the place of kneeling and asking the Lord to show you what you should do. "If any of you lack wisdom," James writes, "let him ask of God, that giveth to all men liberally, and upbraideth not; and it shall be given him" (James 1:5).

Question: Do you do any yardwork? If so, when do you do it?

Answer: Yes, I do yardwork, and I enjoy it. Of course, whether we like it or not, we still have to do it.

My husband usually mows the lawn, even though I have done it for him *many* a time. One of us mows on Thursday afternoon or early evening. On Friday morning, I go out at about eight o'clock and do the trimming. I trim bushes and lawns weekly. The job doesn't take that long if done weekly, and, of course, the outside of the house always looks nice if the trimming is done consistently. In the summer, I water the lawn and shrubs two to three times a week.

Question: Do you have any ideas on how not to lose socks during the washing process? I have a box full of unmatched socks!

Answer: I don't lose many socks. I believe it has something to do with the way I do the wash. I wash, dry, fold, and put it away immediately. I don't let the clothes sit around in a pile for days as people trip over them. I suggest you do the same.

If this doesn't help, try pinning socks together with a safety pin while you sort the laundry. When the clothes come out of the dryer, the socks will still be a pair. You can also put all the socks in a lingerie bag and leave them in the bag during the drying process.

Sometimes during the sorting process, we may skip a sock that's in the bottom of the hamper and think it's lost. If you're missing a sock, look in the bottom of the hamper.

Question: My grandmother, who is not a Seventh-day Adventist, lives with us. Keeping the Sabbath means nothing to her. She watches television during the Sabbath, and our children end up listening to the TV, doing things that I don't want them to do on the Sabbath. What do you suggest?

Answer: I am taking it for granted that you have already asked for her cooperation in this matter. If she refuses, I can see only two options.

Put the TV in her room so she can watch it privately. I would even consider buying a television for her room. With a remote control, she can watch it comfortably.

If this doesn't work, become creative and plan an outing or some fun activity for the family every Sabbath. Try to make the Sabbath so enjoyable and keep your kids so busy they won't be attracted to Grandma's TV.

Question: If your house was a real mess and someone told you by telephone that they would be arriving at your house shortly, what would you do? Where would you start cleaning?

Answer: I would start with the living room, family room, and dining room. I would put everything that did not belong in those rooms in a clothes basket in a corner. After everything was cleared, I would fluff the throw pillows and generally straighten up. Then I would take the clothes basket to my bedroom and put it in a corner somewhere.

I would then move to the kitchen. I would clear all tables and counters and put the dishes in the dishwasher. If I didn't have enough time for all this, I would stack the dishes neatly in the sink. If everything else is tidy, the stacked dishes won't look so bad.

Now I would go into the bathroom, tidy it all up, and spray a disinfectant on the sink and counter. (I would hope that my husband or someone else would have already done the bathroom for me.)

I would do the bedrooms only if I had time. It's easy to just close the bedroom door and hide it from view if necessary.

Question: I would like to get more information on your plans for home management. Can I contact you directly?

Answer: Yes. If you would like more information about parenting, home organization, or seminars on Sabbath preparation, write to me at this address:

Yara C. Young
1682 Pineford Ct.
Stone Mountain, GA 30088

I'll be happy to discuss any additional homemaking questions you might have.

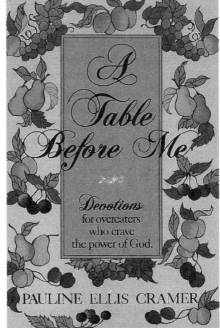

They're Back!

More **Adventist Hot Potatoes** is a continuation of Martin Weber's quest to find balance in the issues that tend to make church members a little hot under the collar.

With charity and an open mind, Weber asks:

- Is Adventist education still a good investment?
- Can anything good come from independent ministries?
- Do Adventist hospitals still promote our health message?
- Did Jesus feel like sinning?

Don't skip this second helping of hot potatoes.

US$8.95/Cdn$10.75. Paper.

To order, call toll free 1-800-765-6955, or visit your local ABC.

Books You Just Can't Put Down